Annie Sloan's

ROOM RECIPES
FOR STYLE AND
COLOR

Annie Sloan's

ROOM RECIPES
FOR STYLE AND
COLOR

Annie Sloan and Felix Sloan

With specially commissioned photography by Christopher Drake

CICO BOOKS
LONDON NEW YORK
www.rylandpeters.com

Published in 2014 by CICO Books
An imprint of Ryland Peters & Small Ltd

20–21 Jockey's Fields   341 E 116th St
London WC1R 4BW   New York, NY 10029
www.rylandpeters.com

10 9 8 7 6 5 4 3 2 1

Text © Annie Sloan and Felix Sloan 2014
Design © CICO Books 2014
Photography © CICO Books and RPS 2014
(Photographs on pages 18 below, 21 above, and 30
© Christopher Drake)

A CIP catalog record for this book is available from the
Library of Congress and the British Library.

US ISBN: 978-1-78249-154-5
UK ISBN: 978-1-78249-171-2

Printed in China

Editor: Dawn Bates
Designer: Louise Leffler
Artworks: Annie Sloan and Felix Sloan
Commissioned photography: Christopher Drake
For further picture credits, see page 220.

In-house editor: Carmel Edmonds
In-house designer: Fahema Khanam
Art director: Sally Powell
Production manager: Gordana Simakovic
Publishing manager: Penny Craig
Publisher: Cindy Richards

contents

INTRODUCTION

Deciding how to style and decorate your home isn't easy. There are so many ways of approaching the task and so many styles to choose from. Like most people, you may worry about making a mistake or lack confidence in your choices. Our room recipes help you decide on the best style for you and give an overview of interior design and home decor. The styles we explore are all quite polarized. They are by no means definitive, but they capture quite specific looks. In reality, most homes are fusions of more than one style but even the most experienced designer will find it difficult to juggle more than two or three styles in one room.

An inspirational journey

This is a world we know well but both Felix's and my preconceptions were jolted in writing this book. Felix was

amazed to find that of all the locations photographed for the book, the most unrestrained—which in that sense made it feel rather modern—was the 17th-century Swedish manor house with its quirky mock picture frames and freely painted panels. For me, the 1960s design of the modern retro location was a real eye-opener. Being at art school in the 1960s, I viewed mainstream design of the time as pedestrian: unchallenging and uninteresting. How wrong I was!

What is a "style"?

We can define a style as being a particular approach or a unified look. This look is like a palette consisting of colors, shapes, cultural and historic references, materials, attitudes, even ideologies. This palette can be drawn upon in many different ways to create a design style. When we describe a room as "stylish," we are saying that all of the elements are balanced and work well together.

The more knowledgeable you are, the better. A broad knowledge is like a repertoire of ideas that you can draw upon. If, for example, you have a chair and you are not sure what to put with it, knowing the style of that chair will give you ideas. It's not about creating a rule book, but more a set of guidelines. If you are inexperienced or lack confidence, you may find that following the style guide in this book helps you. If you are an experienced decorator, you will find that you can make all sorts of style fusions work.

[opposite, above] These pieces are modern retro. The excellence of this design style was a particular revelation to me.

[opposite, center, and below] Swedish style: The quirky freeness of the haphazardly laid hand-painted Chinese wallpaper and the painted faux picture frame and border were an inspiration to Felix.

[above] We both found the painterly approach to French elegance very motivating. Throughout the book, we have suggested paint swatches, such as the greens shown here, for each style.

[right] This sitting room [above] shows a charming and somewhat edgy take on the vintage floral style, while this collection of items [below] is warehouse style in both its look and arrangement.

STORYTELLING

Show homes and hotel rooms are sometimes stunning and inspiring but they are not home. To make a house into a home, you need it to have your personal stamp. Having the things around you that say who you are gives your house individuality and personality.

Personal items might be a toy elephant from childhood, old photographs of family and friends, a postcard of a favorite painting or vacation, souvenirs, an ornament, or maybe a vintage picture you found one weekend. We often have things that we don't want to throw away because they are a part of us. Instead of storing them away, display them and use them to tell your story.

Photographs

Tell your story using photographs. There will be a variety of styles and times your photographs were taken—some will be in color and others in black and white, and some may be very old sepia prints. They can be brought together by using similar frames or by painting frames the same color. For instance, using large frames all painted black gives a cohesive look to the photos. Or placing items on a colored background or putting them together in a strong-shaped frame can unite a mix of finds.

Collectibles

Whatever your interests, from abacuses to zebras, you can use them to tell a story in your home. We are not talking about giving each room a theme. Theming a room is great for a special occasion but not really something you want to live with on a day-to-day basis.

Some people make large collections—for example, antique dolls. This can easily become a big mess of objects that don't particularly work well together, so it's important to connect them in some way. Tim Gosling, whose neoclassical home we visited (see Chapter 1), had a collection of horse ornaments. These worked well together because of their color and shape, and because they fitted in with the style of the room—there was other horse imagery used in the decor.

Almost anything can become interesting when multiples are collected together. The image on the opposite page, below, is of my mantelpiece. I had collected each of these pieces over many years and they were scattered around different parts of my house. When I came to redesign my living room, I needed a collection of objects to go on my gray marble fireplace, so brought them all together. The largest piece is a stone statue given to me by my father. The small figure of a man is, in fact, a maquette for a larger piece. I bought it in China from a modern artist. I found the skull on a beach on a small island in Fiji, the birthplace of my mother. The ammonite is from my garden, and the woman's head is a painted plaster cast from a medieval church in Oxfordshire.

[left] These are the sort of photographs and objects that could just languish in a box in the attic but, brought out and framed, they make a lively display.

[above] Noticeboards, blackboards, and postcards stuck on the wall or the back of a door are a great way to add a personal touch that can constantly evolve and keep pace with your life. Their impermanence means that they can be chopped and changed.

[right] These very personal objects of Annie's, collected over several years, are brought together on her mantelpiece.

DESIGN PRINCIPLES

If everything in a room were the same height, size, color, and texture, there would be nothing for the eye to look at. You need something eye-catching that will lead anyone entering the room to look around. Composition is about creating arrangements—thinking about how you place items, as well as considering the space in between them.

Symmetry and asymmetry

True symmetry requires two facing sides of an arrangement to be exactly identical. This is something that can work very well in certain interiors, and with particular design styles, such as neoclassical (see Chapter 1). However, a lot of the time it is more interesting to use symmetry as a starting point but then break out of it. Balance is such an important requirement in composition, and symmetry helps to provide this.

Let's take the image opposite as an example. At the core of this composition are a few symmetrical elements: the candlesticks, the Edwardian busts, the classical head in the center, and the mirror. The symmetry is broken by various smaller objects along the mantelpiece and, in fact, on closer inspection some of the elements that appear to be symmetrical are not. The candlesticks are different colors, the busts have slightly different poses, the head is tilted to one side, and the mirror has an asymmetrical plume at the top.

Height and scale

The display on this mantelpiece also works well because there is a balance of height and scale. Without the candlesticks, there would be nothing to take the eye from the level of the smaller objects up to the oversized mirror. The larger objects catch your eye at first, and then lead you to look at some of their more detailed features. Finally, you start to notice the tiny objects, such as the delicate cherub. Having a good mix of different levels of detail means that you always have something of interest to look at.

Think of your space in terms of floor level, eye level, and above eye level. You should try to have something of interest in each of these

places. Similarly, you should aim to have a range of different-sized objects in a room, from the large and obvious, down to the small, intimate, and detailed.

Shape

Another way to think about composition is in terms of arrangements of shapes. A shared characteristic, such as shape, will help to bring different elements in a space together, but having too many things the same shape will be rather boring—so, once again, a balanced approach is needed. For instance, the introduction of a round table into a room made up of squares and rectangles could be just the thing to bring the room together.

Taking the image above as an example, the principles used for the arrangement on this chest of drawers are the same as those you would use in a whole room. The setting is made up of two basic shapes: circles and rectangles. The balanced positioning with varying concentrations of action makes it interesting and pleasing to the eye.

[opposite] As well as showing symmetry, the composition in this image is also a great example of the other design principles discussed: height, scale, focus, and storytelling. The colors—Old White, and a little Primer Red against a French Linen wall—are subdued and harmonious, helping to make this a story about the objects on display.

[above] When there is a lack of color in an arrangement, it is even more important for the shapes to work well. Here, everything is in neutral tones, forcing attention on the shapes involved. The circular clock and bowl provide focus and are a terrific counterpoint to the hard, straight edges of the rest of the items.

Focus

Every room needs some sort of focus to bring everything in it together. One key way to think about where the focus of a room should be is by considering viewpoints. A viewpoint could be a place that you often sit, such as an armchair; or a place in the room where you often stand such as the entrance or doorway. In this case the focus becomes a matter of first impressions.

Having worked out where the focus point is in the room, consider what to feature there, drawing on the other design principles. For example, you may choose to add an element of storytelling, through hanging pictures or paintings, or introduce scale, through a large object such as a chandelier. You may even use colors as your focus, whether they blend together or contract with each other.

[above] Despite being a quiet corner behind a cupboard, this intimate space is the first thing you see when entering the kitchen from the dining room. This makes it an important viewpoint in the room and therefore a perfect place to hang some strong, interesting pictures.

[right] This view takes you across three rooms. The pink on the walls of the first and last rooms leads your eye through the middle room. There is strong Scandinavian Pink at one end, and the subtler pink of Antoinette at the front.

[opposite] This chandelier makes a huge statement in a large, tall, open-plan room, and helps you anchor your eye before taking in the rest of the surroundings. While everything else is quite practical, the chandelier, along with the giant fork, offers some change by being a little frivolous and unusual.

STYLE FUSIONS

Most people's homes do not adhere to one particular style. Everyone develops an individual style by fusing their favorite elements from different sources. This is one key way to bring some personal identity to the design of your home. You should not be put off from buying things that you like just because they don't fit in with one particular style. Collect things that you are naturally drawn to, and you should be able to find ways to put them together.

Color is a great way of bringing together disparate elements. This could, of course, be a collection of objects that are all the same colors—black and white, or all yellow, for example. Another way to use color to bring elements together is with a color scheme. For example, a modern abstract painting on a wall could play off antique furniture in the same room if it used colors that tie in.

You may find that some objects of very different styles happen to be similar shapes and therefore work nicely together. Juxtaposing strongly contrasting styles is a playful way of creating a fusion. An interesting counterpoint to a rustic setting could be to have some very grand elements, for example.

In this book, some of the locations are, in fact, fusions rather than pure styles. Paul Massey's coastal haven (see Chapter 8) incorporates many warehouse elements (see Chapter 9). Alex Russell Flint's house in France (see Chapter 6) has an eccentric bohemian layer to it, while our bohemian location (see Chapter 4) was fused with a little vintage floral (see Chapter 5). The modern retro (see Chapter 3) and neoclassical (see Chapter 1) locations, for example, were very much the work of purists.

[opposite] This room is essentially based on three different styles. The architecture of the space is in the warehouse style, with its exposed steel beams and corrugated ceiling; the painted doors, chandelier, and armchairs are all very much French elegance; the large sofa, coffee table, and floor lamp are all modern retro elements. These seemingly disparate elements are all balanced by good composition. If you were to add any more style elements, it would be very hard to stop the room becoming cluttered and confused.

[top] A random collection of objects gathered together, next to a cabriole leg. They work together nicely by being a mix of square and curvy shapes.

[right] A French armchair sits next to a mid-century side table, topped with some Chinese figures and a modern artwork.

Chapter 1

NEOCLASSICAL

If you want to make a grand statement in your home, look no further than neoclassical. We particularly love this style for its precision, its focus on strong imagery, and its "wow" factor. While neoclassical won't necessarily work everywhere, it is easy to introduce elements of it into your home. It is a style that is always referencing back, but there is something timeless—something classic and charming—about it.

"Classical" refers to the ancient art and architecture of Greece and the Roman Empire, and also to China. "Neoclassical" simply means a revival of interest in what is still considered a "golden age." For great examples of classical architecture, think of the Parthenon in Athens or the Colosseum in Rome—picture those classic columns. For a more modern example, look at the White House—inside and out, the U.S. President resides in a neoclassical building.

The first flowering of the neoclassical style was in the late 18th and early 19th centuries. During this Georgian era, architecture, in a sense, came indoors to show off all the simple geometric forms of classic style, through furniture, furnishings, moldings, decorative materials, drawings, and statues. For example, a Doric column (see page 23) could become anything from a wallpaper motif to a chair leg or lamp base. Neoclassical is also about order and symmetry, a sense of space and balance, and a certain amount of regimentation.

[opposite] Look at this room's composition and imagery. Classical antiquity is referenced in the use of the busts, the obelisk, and the architectural drawings. Meanwhile, the door features bas-reliefs of robed women, and the marble mantelpiece an urn—both are good examples of neoclassical imagery.

[above] Classical architecture comes indoors with a pediment-topped portico sitting on a gilt-bordered door. Symmetry and formality are enhanced by the bookshelves, set in column form and topped with Roman busts. The gilt cornice is classic too.

elements of NEOCLASSICAL style

Colors and materials

The colors favored in the neoclassical style tend to exude a strong, positive presence. There is nothing "flowery" about them. Pretty pastels feature only in a context where they appear powerful—i.e., alongside white—or where they are reinforced by stronger, darker colors.

The Georgian neoclassical revival coincided with the Industrial Revolution and developments in science, which saw the production of bold new pigments, such as ultramarine, cobalt blue, and chrome yellow. These pigments were soon seen on the smartest drawing-room walls and furniture in 19th-century London. My own new Napoleonic Blue color (see opposite) is inspired by the French emperor and his love of neoclassical design. It is a regal color—a deep, warm blue. It contains a hint of red, so it makes

great purples when mixed with other paint colors. Purple is considered very much an Ancient Roman color, as Roman emperors wore purple.

Decorative stone features prominently as a material in the neoclassical style, with granite, marble, and travertine being particular favorites. Again, this references the first great neoclassical revival, which put the stones of antiquity into the limelight in Europe and in North America too. Proportions and styles were modeled on Greek and Roman architecture, and decorative stones were fundamentally important to the ornamentation. Plaster is also widely used with plaster casts and plaster walls. Shiny metals, traditionally gold leaf, brass, polished bronze, and silver, are neoclassical materials, but modern interpretations include stainless steel and chrome, as well as glass and mirrors.

[above] The paint effect on this cabinet mimics malachite, a mineral with an emerald green, coppery color. The mirror is topped by a gilded imperial-style eagle, which is very neoclassical, as are the brass lion and candlesticks.

[left] The gilded cornice is shown to great effect against the regal purple. You can get close to this color using Burgundy and Napoleonic Blue.

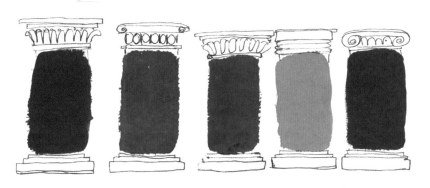

My mini columns show a palette of five classic "imperial" colors. From left to right: Burgundy, Aubusson Blue, Napoleonic Blue, a purple mix using Napoleonic Blue, Burgundy, and Old White, and a deeper purple mix with the same combination but no white.

My illustration is all about composition and symmetry. Regularity, especially using columns and other motifs in pairs, is a neoclassical look. Even the chair provides a symmetry of viewpoint, and everything is lined up.

Arrangement and furniture

Neoclassical style works best when there is space and symmetry. It is framed around order and balance, and there is a certain military precision to the setup of its interiors (not surprising given these empires of antiquity were massive military powers). Panels and columns mimic the formation of Greek or Roman troops in battle. Architecture, too, influences the arrangements, which tend to be columnar, square, rectangular, or triangular.

Other militaristic elements include symbols of war and victory, such as classical palm leaves and laurel wreaths. These symbols often enveloped other imagery and made a direct visual connection back to the power of the Ancient Roman emperors. Other plant arrangements often associated with the neoclassical style include the acanthus leaf, symmetrical box balls, and individual plants that need arranging or trimming into a structured shape or that lend themselves to topiary.

[top] A detail of the cabinet (see opposite, top). First, I painted it in Graphite. Over the tabletop, I put a layer of Florence—a bluey-green color inspired by malachite. Then, when it was dry, I varnished the table with lacquer. Next, I painted Aubusson Blue all over the top, creating the finish with some strips from corrugated card. I "combed" them over the surface, pulling, curling, and turning them to create fan shapes.

The idea of trying to make a piece of furniture resemble a scale model of a building underlines every revival of classicism—from the Renaissance to the 1980s to contemporary twists. The Renaissance was inspired by classical antiquity, and from that period onward the ancient ruins were excavated and studied for the secrets of classical beauty. Classical architecture became the direct reference for neoclassical furniture and interiors, as little firsthand evidence remained, apart from the ancient buildings themselves. So obelisks, columns, and plinths, for example, became chair and table legs, lamp bases, and door frames. The chief reference was the Ancient Greek and Roman ornamental Doric

[above] These three chairs were designed by Tim Gosling (see page 24) and are modernized versions of traditionally shaped pieces. The "gondola" chair [left] features a classic architectural drawing design (for a more traditional gondola chair, including the swan armrest so beloved by Empress Josephine, see page 22). The red and white leather padded chairs [center and right] are modernist takes on neoclassical styles.

[below] I drew these chair designs with Regency stripes, and added a palette of greens. From left to right: Antibes Green, Antibes Green with Old White, Provence, Old Violet, and Florence.

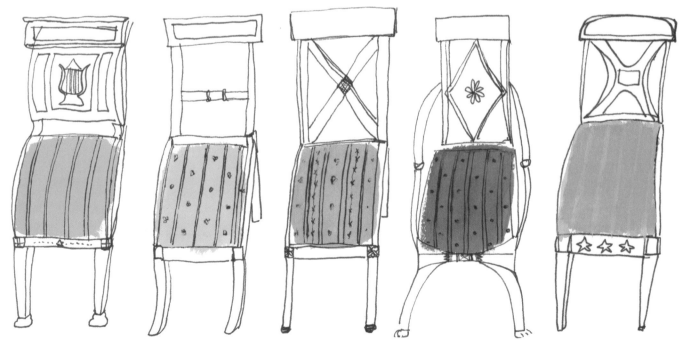

column. This is made up of a pedestal and plinth at the base, supporting the main column or shaft, and topped by architraves, friezes, and cornices. Accordingly, you will find miniature columns on freestanding furniture, especially chair and table legs, as well as on bookcases, lamp bases, door and window frames, interior walls, fireplaces, and door panels. Fixtures and fittings, including dado rails, baseboards (skirting boards), architraves, and cornices, are pretty much defined by moldings in the neoclassical style.

Neoclassical furniture is really any piece that has an added classic architectural element or material. It might be chair legs modeled on Ancient Greek columns or a dressing-table mirror supported by obelisk-shaped stands. Popular pieces of neoclassical furniture include the chaise longue—often depicted in scenes from antiquity on murals. These "long chairs" could consist of two parts with a large stool. They are based on the daybed often pictured in Ancient Greek and Roman scenes.

Consoles, which are basically any type of wall table, are also popular. Originally, a console might be fixed to the wall and supported only by the front legs or an eagle or other figure. Wall tables allow you to display an attractive collection of ornaments.

[above] Gold, the predominant theme around this fireplace, helps to maximize the amount of reflective surfaces. Urns—the vase-shaped vessels often seen as a motif in Greco-Roman carving—have been used as a classical decorative feature since Renaissance times. This pair of gilded urns, set on onyx plinths and standing guard in front of the gilt-framed mirror, are from the Napoleonic Empire period.

I found this French gilt-framed mirror in a junk shop. The bust was a rather awful, mass-produced terracotta find but I dabbed it with Paris Grey and Old White to give it a marbled look. Purple lilies complete the formal arrangement.

Ancient imagery and collectibles

There are plenty of places to source classic ornaments—from junk shops to reproduction furniture websites. It is very satisfying to find items such as a small bust, a Roman-style terracotta planter, or a Greek-style statuette in a reclamation store. Obvious ornaments include reproduction Roman or Greek busts and statuettes of women in robes.

If you are feeling creative, you can make your own plaster pieces, such as a molding. However, simply collecting items that feature Ancient Roman or Greek imagery, like old architectural prints, puts you within the tradition of neoclassicism. It is really the imagery that's important, so reproductions of frescoes, and measured drawings of classical temples, theaters, mausoleums, and sculptures will all do nicely. Key imagery includes laurel and acanthus, egg-and-dart (see page 32), oak leaves and Greek palm leaves, swans, lyres, urns, and wreaths.

For inspiration, visit your nearest museum or museum of art or look at the websites of national galleries and museums. It could be your version of the 19th-century "grand tour," when wealthy travelers visited the museums, monuments, and temples of antiquity of Europe. The neoclassical style arose from the firsthand observation of these tourists, and reproduction of the works of antiquity came to dominate the decorative arts of England, Europe, and America in the late 18th century.

If you are collecting neoclassical pieces, the ornament or furniture can happily be fake because you can create a paint effect to make it look real. Try to find an alternative material to marble, such as resin or terracotta, and then paint it by dabbing and stippling (adding small spots with the tips of the bristles) to give it an antique feel (as I did with the bust on page 21).

[above] This collection of ornaments includes some Mediterranean coral. You don't have to collect authentic artifacts—try sourcing old or worn items, then paint them or add a faux finish.

This illustration is based on a gondola chair that was supplied for Empress Josephine's boudoir. The swan was her Napoleonic emblem, representing fidelity. It was often used to decorate armrests or formed the entire arms of a chair.

[right] This selection of plaster busts is set on a decorative stone table supported by Doric column table legs.

[below] These plaster moldings, busts, and statuettes are in the classical revivalist style. Any imagery that depicts something classical is relevant to the neoclassical style.

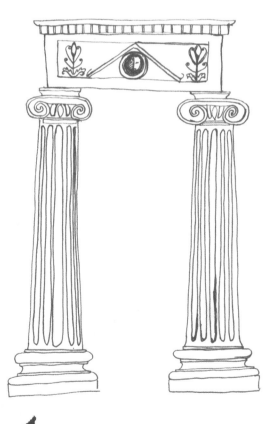

This illustration is my take on Ancient Greek/Roman ornamental Doric columns. They are made up of a pedestal and plinth at the base, supporting the main column or shaft, and topped by an architrave with friezes and cornices. Both Greek and Roman architecture featured the Doric, Ionic, and Corinthian columns. There were exact rules about proportions and profiles of each surface, molding, and ornament.

A LONDON APARTMENT

We were delighted to discover this magnificent apartment in a large three-story, double-fronted house built in the late 18th century. It is owned by Tim Gosling, a furniture designer in the neoclassical tradition. The building started out as a private residence but has been through many uses since; at one time it was a school. Now it is used for living once again, and Tim has an apartment and a design studio in the building. Both have become a wonderful canvas for his work.

Tim draws heavily on classical architecture and 17th- and 18th-century British architects such as Inigo Jones, the Adam brothers, Robert and James, William Kent, and Sir Christopher Wren. The vocabulary that Tim uses to design his apartment and furniture is the imagery, architecture, and art of the ancient world, calling on Ancient Rome, Greece, and Egypt. He cleverly achieves a modern, updated, clean, and unfussy look.

There are many wonderful features in this apartment but Tim's "Plaster Room" left us speechless. It displays his collection of plaster casts bought at auctions and through friends. The most spectacular is the copy of a famous statue of a discus thrower, shown opposite. This has been placed in front of the arched plaster niche, called an apse, which would once have contained a sideboard. All the plasterwork is original and now lovingly restored and gilded in the most magnificent and dramatic way.

Mathematical, almost absolute symmetry, along with cubic, rectangular, or geometric shapes, and symbols of military power all come together in this setting.

There are numerous types of stencils that can help you create neoclassical symmetrical imagery, like the double-headed eagle shown here. Even the *Vitruvian Man* can be sourced as a stencil. To stop the stencil having a folk-art finish, the image should be applied very flatly, perhaps with a roller, to make it completely even.

SYMMETRY SYMMETRY

We both liked the dining room very much, although we only found out later that it was added onto by Tim to make it a perfect square. This may have been why it felt so "right." The room has many references to both hidden and obvious symmetry but it is never rigidly adhered to.

Enlarging the room by pushing out also allowed for the addition of the oculi—the round-shaped niches that hold the Roman busts (see page 29). These give the room such character and individuality, especially when they are lit from behind in the evenings.

The decoration and paintwork in this room are very inspiring, from the painted frieze to the gilding and the panel of gray paint behind the oculi. This entire room has the same white, black, and gold color palette as the others in the apartment, but here there is a strong yellow, an earthy red for the gilding, and also a wonderful Roman purple used on the fabric of the chairs.

[opposite] Two, tall, gilded Napoleonic urns frame a collection of classic horse statuettes, from an 8th-century Chinese horse to contemporary Clapham Pottery designs. The horse motif continues with the painted frieze, which is set on a gilded background and complemented by the gilded framework of the main painting. That painting is a copy, by owner Tim Gosling, of a 19th-century painting full of classical references called *The Lament for Icarus* by Herbert James Draper.

[above] In the center of the dining room is a large round table that was designed by Tim specifically for the space. The double-headed eagle design is inlaid with brass into ebony, a technique historically described as "boulle work." The design was taken from a set of wine glasses that Tim brought back from St. Petersburg. The eagle, or *aquila*, was a symbol of the Roman army, and can be seen in different forms on all sorts of military designs. On the table is an open book showing Leonardo da Vinci's *Vitruvian Man*, an iconic and hugely influential Renaissance homage to the Roman architect Vitruvius.

[opposite] Neoclassical design is influenced by a mixture of different ancient civilizations. Taking inspiration from the Ancient Egyptian temple Karnak, Tim designed this fireplace with tapered uprights and a massive curved overmantel. The assembly of objects on the mantelpiece is a mixture of modern, Ancient Egyptian, Ancient Chinese, and Napoleonic. This combination works because the layout is so precise, and the different items have a common theme, such as horses, which are a popular subject matter in the classical tradition.

[right] This hand-painted gray panel is a clever design device. It brings order to the wall by determining a central point, reinforcing the symmetry of the curtains and the crosses above them. Another skillful device is the niche. Round niches, known as oculi, have their origins in Roman architecture, and were common in Renaissance Italy.

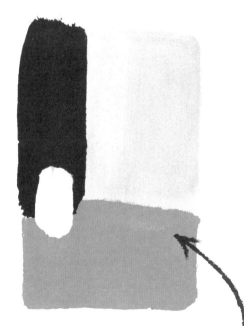

This is my swatch for the painted frieze color scheme consisting of black, white, and gray, with a yellow background.

Balanced and symmetrical arrangements with different heights can be seen throughout Tim's very well designed and proportioned apartment. This meticulous attention to detail is partly what makes this a perfect example of neoclassical style. The eye is led around the room and always has somewhere to focus.

CLEVER **DECOR**

We love the way Tim has applied a panel of paint behind the niches to give them definition and emphasize them, as if they are part of a column. Painting a wall in this way is something that could be used more in decorating, as it helps to give height and definition to a room. The decoration on the cornice, the frieze, and the ribboned cross molding is one of the highlights of the room. The painted frieze (see overleaf) is a huge amount of work but it is absolutely worth it. Drawing the eye to the different heights is not always easy, especially in a small room, but it has been done very well by Tim.

On the mantelpiece is a delightfully quirky collection of horses—an 8th-century Tang horse in the center, with modern horses from Clapham Pottery between two tall Napoleonic gilded ceramic urns.

Leading off the dining room is the bedroom, where you are presented with an impressive, 13ft- (4m-) high contemporary fourposter designed by Tim. Placed in the center of the room, it is made of mahogany using posts from a piece of furniture he found in Barbados. The bed head is inlaid with a silver border. The colors are minimal—just whites, silver, and mahogany brown, plus the gold of the picture frame and the red on the pillowcases.

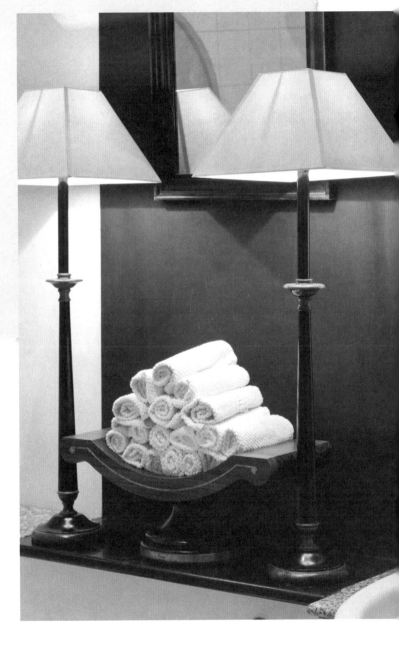

[opposite] Although there are modern elements in this bedroom, there is a lot that ties it to the neoclassical tradition. The white cushions have a red key pattern, which is typical of Ancient Greek design. The inclusion of architectural elements, such as a niche, is very neoclassical, as is the stylish, symmetrical layout.

[above] The scroll is an extremely prevalent motif in neoclassical design. It is seen on furniture, on the tops of columns, and in patterns. Here, in the bathroom, Tim has hinted at this motif with his orderly towel arrangement. The wooden dish that holds the towels even includes a simplified version of the scroll motif on each end. The whole setting with the lamps is balanced beautifully by symmetry.

OLD MEETS **NEW**

We found the drawing room to be a wonderful mix of grandeur and comfort, classic and modern, and it is a tour de force in interior-design skills. The result is a magnificent room that achieves character, warmth, and presence.

The huge painting, a copy of a 19th-century work called *The Lament for Icarus*—a popular classical story—by Herbert James Draper, caught our eye immediately because it commandingly sets the mood and the focus of the room. None of the original fireplaces had survived in the apartment, so Tim was able to accommodate the painting and then design a contemporary fireplace underneath it. The fireplace has a stone slab supported by two 18th-century gilded corbel brackets that came out of a French chateau.

The cornices, with urns and a floral garland, are original to the building and have been restored and gilded. To keep the ceiling uncluttered with lights, Tim came up with a great plan. He ran a mahogany border around the entire edge of the street-level reception rooms and put in uplighters that reflect off the ceiling, giving all the rooms a soft, even spread of light with minimum shadowing. The lights also bring to life all the gilding in the room as well as the mirrored doors.

The mirrored doors either side of the fireplace add elegance and light. Originally, the doors on the right were false, leading nowhere, and just acted as mirrors to reflect light and give a feeling of space. When the building next door became available, Tim was able to extend into that room and make it his dining room.

On the left of the room is a long bookcase painted white, with mahogany pillars. Either side of the central door, Tim has placed two plaster columns. A pediment with a griffin design gives height to the low door and to the room. In contrast to all the straight lines elsewhere, the sofas are soft and comfortable.

This is my take on Tim's drawing-room cornice. The horizontal group of moldings in this room, as with all cornices, represents the top of the Doric column. Notice the "egg-and-dart" (or round and pointy) motif, which is one of the most common carved enrichments in the neoclassical style. You can buy such moldings as new or as wallpaper designs or a frieze, or you could source an actual one. I've added the acanthus-style plant motif, again a popular neoclassical feature.

[opposite] Light plays a leading role in the theatrical design of this interior. Upward-pointing lights are set into the floor to illuminate the moldings in the ceiling and show off their gilded details to maximum effect. The mirrors in the doors create the sense of a continuous, flowing space, even when they are shut. Gold helps to maximize the amount of reflective surfaces. Both the gilded edges of the mirror panels and the late 18th-century gilded plaster cornice under the picture bring a warm brilliance to the space.

[overleaf] This spectacular sitting room is not just for show—it's a space to relax in, with a piano, a television, and comfortable sofas. The sense of grandeur has been created with the huge classical painting in the center and the architectural embellishments. The small door on the left of the room has been transformed with the addition of large, white pillars and a pediment. It is flanked on either side by two identical bookcases with mahogany pillars.

compared to the larger, brass sheets, which are imitation gold. The process is the same, so paint the glue (called gold size) to the areas where you want there to be gold. For best results, sprinkle talcum powder onto the surface before you apply the size.

Once the gold size is transparent, it is ready for the leaf to be applied. It will be sticky but not wet. It does not need to be sealed, but imitation gold (brass) does, as it is much shinier. Apply clear wax over the top for a finish that is the same as real gold—brass is rather shiny in comparison.

The frieze shown opposite was done on a strip of fine canvas and painted before being glued to the wall. It is hand-painted in black and white, and hand-gilded on a yellow background. It's a scale copy of the Elgin Marbles frieze that was made into a wallpaper in the 19th century but is no longer available.

Creating this frieze does require you to be able to draw, but something similar could be done using decoupage figures, photocopied as a paper strip, enlarged to fit, and glued down, with the background then painted yellow.

Alternatively, the separate figures could be copied and cut out and then glued down to fit a space. It does not have to be an exact copy of the Elgin Marbles, especially if the design is done on the cornice of a cupboard or on a chest of drawers.

[above, left] All around the door moldings, gold size has been added and then leaf applied on top. The effect is very regal.

[opposite, above] This magnificent frieze is typical of the neoclassical period. The horse theme is used throughout the apartment.

Gilding

To give your home a neoclassical look, simply apply gilding to molded surfaces, such as door panels, or to the cornices. For a more challenging project, create a neoclassical frieze in the style of the one shown on the opposite page.

There are several ways to apply gold leaf to a surface. Real gold in transfer form is the most realistic and shiny. It is lightly adhered to a fine tissue, so it can be handled and transferred to a sticky surface. Real gold comes in small sheets and is relatively expensive

Here is my sample of designs for moldings that could be hand-painted or stencilled to look like solid objects, especially along friezes and borders. Draw them first and apply gold size, then leaf, to the shapes to make neoclassical images.

Chapter 2

TRADITIONAL SWEDISH

Swedish style is, in our opinion, the first and last word in painted furniture. It has been a huge influence on my work because of its long association with paintwork, not just on furniture, but in the all-wooden interiors that say "Sweden."

This distinctively cool and charming style blends a unique mixture of rustic farmhouse with grand chateaux. It exudes a gorgeous, painterly quality over uncluttered interiors and stripped-back finishes. It is also a "recipe" that is extremely achievable for any would-be decorator.

The style is also known as Gustavian, after Gustav III, who ruled Sweden when it was punching its weight with both France and Russia in the late 18th century. Inspired by a visit to the Palace of Versailles, he adopted the French neoclassical decor but gave it a Swedish twist. It was a regal, stately but subdued style, with Prussian blue (then a new and expensive color) used alongside whites and light grays, gilded finishes on large mirrors (to give more light in winter), chandeliers, and lime-washed floorboards.

The look became more rustic as the style moved down the social scale and out to the country. For the provincial version, instead of silk, there was linen, and wooden wall sconces replaced chandeliers. At both ends of the scale, Swedish homes, being typically all-timbered, were painted pale white, with stronger local pigments.

[opposite] This bulbous, long-case clock is known as a Mora, after the town where these hourglass-shaped timepieces were first made. It is a classic of the traditional Swedish farmhouse style, as is the wall candleholder.

[above] Two typically pared-back versions of French neoclassical chairs show rectangular backings linked by graceful, curved crosses.

elements of TRADITIONAL SWEDISH style

Stylish furniture

When it comes to furniture, the Gustavian style is essentially a pared-down version of French neoclassicism: less formal, more relaxed, and prettier. It is also greatly enhanced by the use of distressed paintwork (see overleaf) and the mix of those beautiful, earthy Scandinavian hues. The legs on tables, chairs, and sofas are often carved with scallop detailing, plus a wheatsheaf or rosette at the top—it is a more rustic look than you would get in straightforward neoclassical pieces of furniture.

Sweden is blessed with an abundance of wood from its pine forests. Itinerant painters would travel around the country using the local color palette to paint furniture and rooms in return for food and lodging. They were skilled at faux techniques too—chief among them was distressing paint. Large check or gingham designs proved popular and resulted in a great fusion of quite grand classic shapes with farmhouse-style upholstery (as with the chair, below right).

Traditional Swedish style should not be confused with Swedish modern style (mid-20th century), which simplified the Swedish rendition of neoclassical even further. Its straightforward outlines and a lack of applied ornament fit into most unstylized rooms. This more modern style uses light, plain woods (often pine) in simple curves and roundings, with tapered feet and flat turnings.

Contemporary mass-market Swedish furniture design often goes back to Gustavian roots for its chair and storage design inspiration. Modern furniture outlets, as well as antique fairs and junk shops, can be a good source for Swedish-style pieces.

There is much more to traditional Swedish furniture than simply chairs, though. It's also about secretaires, armoires, and "stepped" bookcases, where the bottom shelf has more depth than the middle and top shelves (see page 48).

As the style filtered to rural areas, the neoclassical, Gustavian motifs were pleasingly adapted for simple pine chests, and beds and cupboards, with plenty of natural pigments and some carving freely used on any flat areas.

A close-up of a traditional Swedish-style chair, in the simplified neoclassical style. It was Gustav III who brought back French chateau inspirations to Swedish palaces after a visit to Versailles. The style filtered down to townhouses and later to farmhouses, where it merged with the tradition of Swedish itinerant interior painters into a more rustic, rough-and-ready, and distressed look.

[opposite, above] The gilt-framed Venetian glass with a candle sconce is typical of the traditional Swedish style.

[opposite, below] The simple side chair has a classic Scandinavian red-and-white gingham check design.

[above] This wooden, decorative country-style piece of Swedish furniture would have been found in a large manor house and painted in blue, gray, or white.

[far left] Many Swedish sofas are neoclassical in style and inspiration—long, arc-shaped arms with a simple crest at the back. These would often be painted in gray-greens and whites, with attention paintwork on the front border.

[left] The secretaire was a popular piece, often painted in a darker color, like this deep blue, while the inside was normally painted either in a pale color, such as gray, or a strong, contrasting color—for instance, the famous Swedish pink.

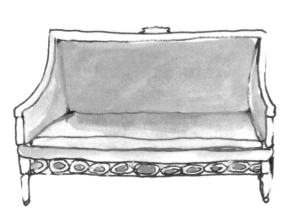

Several different types of paintwork all add up to create a laid-back, bare, uneven texturing look. The freehand paintwork provides a clever, loose, fairly muted green-gray color scheme. Everything is painted here: the walls, floor, doors, and ceiling.

This garland (inset) of white flowers and green foliage provides a simple Swedish, bucolic motif.

Distressed paintwork

Swedish painting style and techniques, particularly the texturing and distressed look that is so recognizable, have guided both of us to great results in our decorative pursuits.

The fashion for the slightly distressed painted look on furniture and paneling emerged from the Gustavian period of the 1780s. Traditionally in Europe, but especially in Sweden, traveling painters would decorate the walls and furniture of the best room in the home in traditional scenes and patterns, in return for a small payment and their board and lodging. They may have started in the royal palaces of Stockholm but they soon moved to well-to-do townhouses and rural farmsteads, adapting their paint colors according to the availability of local pigments.

Stencils to create decorative designs and borders and other faux effects were also used, and the paintwork they employed was extraordinarily imaginative. They painted not just to cover things for practicality but also to create idealized scenes, or to mark an occasion for a room such as a Christening or Christmas. Walls were also painted to imitate silk, hand-printed wallpaper, or marble.

One of the paints they used a lot in Sweden to decorate walls and furniture was egg tempera (a mixture of egg and pigment that was sometimes also mixed with linseed oil). The texture is simply beautiful, almost uneven, with a very slight sheen—and it is hard and durable, and almost waterproof. It's also more permanent than oil paint and dries to a very robust finish, which then toughens over the years, seemingly at odds with its soft, delicate, and flat-matte look.

Because Sweden is blessed with so much natural wood, literally just about everything could be painted—walls, floors, furniture, furnishings—and it was, along with imitations of the moldings and carvings from the French neoclassical style. This merging of ethnic Swedish materials, craftsmen, and creativity with French style led to a highly distinctive distressed paintwork look that is much admired and copied today.

There are so many ways you can age and distress furniture using my paint, but the simplest is often copying the Swedish style by painting and lacquering, and then sanding and applying washes of Old White and Paris Grey to give just the right look.

As for painting wooden floors, the traditional Swedish style involved using lye, which is a very strong alkali made from potash. It was used with soap to clean and bleach, as well as soften and lighten the wood's appearance. With a large brush, a damp sponge, a bucket of water, and my Old White paint, you can achieve a similar, worn look on your wooden floors.

These three examples of Swedish-style paintwork show the muted, pale, light colors and textures that heighten the rough, distressed feel of the surfaces. The paint on the door panels has been literally daubed on in splashes rather than finely executed, and the gilding is distressed, making the whole aspect really charming.

The use of dark and light also adds to the unevenness and the layering effects, which look lovely. It's clever because the surfaces are rougher the closer you look at them. The chair back has simple carving and the paint has come off in areas, so the detail is brought out. Nothing is overworked here—it is very rustic in feel.

The walls were painted in many traditional Swedish manor houses and farmhouses. This example was painted on canvas and then attached to the wall. Something similar could be done by using a stencil for the basic shapes and design, and then elaborating and filling in the detail with looser, freehand painting.

Color combinations

The Swedish color palette is a fascinating mix of muted whites, blues, and classic greens, combined with rich earth reds and yellows—sometimes enlivened with gilded decoration—all over the walls, ceilings, woodwork, and furniture. Other neutral hues traditionally used include putty colors, and off-whites mixed with umber.

The red pigment derives from a deep red oxblood pigment, Falun, named for a region in central Sweden that was at one time the world's largest copper mine. It provided a great source of wealth in the 18th century, which Gustav III used to help make Sweden a leading European power.

The Swedish artist Carl Larrson and his wife Karin created the epitome of the rustic Swedish style with their timber cottage Lilla Hyttnäs, featured in many of his beautiful paintings. The cottage was near Falun, and the artist used both this color and other local pigments as the backdrop for his paintings. Poorer farmers and laborers painted their all-timber cottages in this color because it was a good wood preserver, as well as waterproof. Today, many Swedish country houses are painted with Falun red. Both Falun red and a yellowy ocher, found locally, were used more outside. These earthy, rustic farmhouse colors formed one end of the traditional Swedish color spectrum.

When you add white to my version of Falun, Primer Red, which is a classic color and especially good underneath gilding—so ideal for the traditional Swedish look—it becomes the fabulous Scandinavian Pink. My Swedish pink mimics the slightly purplish-pink of the naturally mixed earthy pinks due to the manganese present in the soil. This is also for us the most "non-pink" because it has no baby girl pink. It also contrasts well with Old White.

Mild, gray-green was a popular color in Gustav's time. It gives a soothing, subdued feel, and is often used in bedrooms. I've referenced it with my own Chateau Grey. By contrast, the bright Prussian blue seen in the palaces of Stockholm implied status because a large quantity of pigment was needed to yield strong colors (this blue was very expensive). My Aubusson Blue and Napoleonic Blue can be used to make traditional colors for Swedish interiors. So, Swedish colors have been hugely influential on my palette—my Paris Grey also comes directly from Sweden.

(left) Three examples of border or panel patterns that work well with traditional Swedish style. Panels are an important way of delineating walls, usually with a combination of patterns and lines.

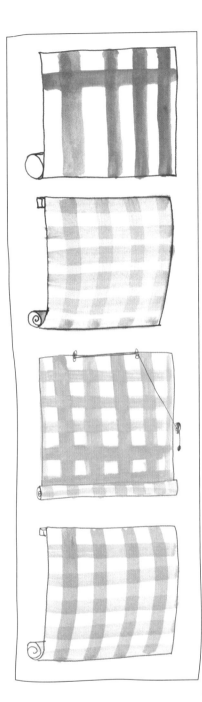

Four patterns for a window blind, which I've done in gingham because that is a very simple, Swedish look.

[right] A typical Swedish country dining room with a simple rustic bench and chairs. Adding to the setting are the candles on the table and the woven rug.

SWEDISH MANOR HOUSE

Our overall impression of Stola Manor, a charming pale pink stone manor house located in the middle of beautiful rolling countryside in southwest Sweden, was how beautifully it worked as a whole. It encompasses many styles but they flow seamlessly from room to room. This is probably because the palette is restrained and within a range of the pigments available at the time.

Stola Manor was in the hands of the same aristocratic family, the Ekeblads, for 400 years, but it is now owned by a trust and not lived in, except by very proud caretakers. Its heyday was during the 18th century, when much of the decorating and most of the changes were made to the house.

In true Swedish style, this house is painted! Paint is everywhere from the whitewashed ceilings and floors, to the hand-painted motifs on the walls and doors and, of course, on the furniture. The colors are not just white and light gray, for which Sweden is famous, but there are blues, pinks, brick reds, and greens too, both in pale and deep shades.

The many styles in this house include bold and hearty baroque, Chinese painted wallpaper, and finely painted wall decorations, as well as gilded rococo. The house was progressively decorated, starting with the more traditional Swedish country style and ending with an international style, such as that in the French-influenced white and gold room.

This 17th-century bookcase is older than the house itself. The classic design, with its step-shape side panels, can still be found in modern Swedish homes. It is painted a soft blue-gray that is very similar to my Paris Grey.

FIRST **IMPRESSIONS**

You enter the middle of the house through impressive doors into a stone-floored hall with wide, gray, washed wooden ceilings and uneven textured walls, painted in soft grayed-white with discernible but subtle brush marks. Incised on the stone wall is 1715, which was when the house was modernized. The lower part of the wall is painted in a deep, warm earth red color, again uneven, topped with a thin, gray-black line. This continues up the low, raised stone staircase, which takes you to the next floor. This is where the house really begins, with a long hallway that runs along part of the front of the house.

The floor is wide wooden planking that has been bleached white, probably done using the traditional Swedish lye soap technique (the lye, a type of bleach, is mixed with caustic lime and white pigments). I have achieved a similar look using Old White, heavily diluted and then washed on with a sponge. This is fine on old floorboards but the technique may be less successful on new wooden boards—yellow sap marks may come through after a year or so. The ceiling also has similar wide planks washed in gray.

[previous page] Stola Manor has a unique style consisting of three mainstays of 17th-century Swedish design. The reddish-brown color on the walls is typical of Swedish rural cottages and barns. Known as Falun red, it is made using red-oxide earth from copper mines. The rustic texture of the paintwork on the wall works beautifully as a contrast to the grand neoclassical busts and the glimpse of rococo prettiness through the open door.

Many of the doors on this floor are painted in an earthy gray-green similar to my Chateau Grey, with very unusual panels of a complex three-dimensional-looking key pattern. It has been painted with a very inspiring loose confidence, which makes it lively and interesting. This key pattern is found on the ceiling of the large central room, albeit in a lighter color and running along the border of the room.

One of the great joys of this house is the way the windows have been treated. There are no curtains, just simple Swedish blinds in large, green checks, and many of the panels around the windows have been painted with a simple landscape of a tree and some grass, each one different and each one a delight.

[above, left] The hand-painted pastoral scenes on the recessed panels are part of the charm of Stola Manor. In keeping with the rural subject matter of these window panels, the paintwork is far from fine. It is unlikely to have been the work of a full-time professional. The paint has been daubed on in layers, with plenty of visible brush strokes. This impressionistic mark gives it a look that would not be out of place in a modern interior.

[above, right] As in a lot of Stola Manor, the paintwork on this door panel is loose and not too perfect—yet it is a delight. We found it reassuring to know that tight perfectionism is not necessary. It is hard to determine the origin of the geometric interlace pattern of this design. It could have its roots in the folk tradition of Nordic knot patterns and, in keeping with the many neoclassical elements in the house, it may have been inspired by Ancient Greek and Roman key patterns. Similar meandering patterns are also found in Chinese design, which was very popular in Europe at this time.

COMBINED STYLES

As we entered the drawing room, we were met by a completely different style from the others in the rest of the house. It's the most French-inspired room and yet, for many, it is quintessentially Swedish too. It was designed by Carl Hårleman, an architect with regal credentials, having worked for the Swedish royal family. Sweden's admiration of French rococo decoration led to the style being distilled and intensified, evolving into a distinctly Swedish look.

It's an inspiring mixture of neoclassical restrained symmetry with rococo asymmetry and frivolity. The walls are all completely paneled and painted in a matte old white with deep-colored gold on the molding. There are two pairs of perfectly proportioned double doors in the corners of the room, echoing the tall panels, with two matching false doors to balance the room. There is classical imagery, such as wreaths and urns. To soften this, there are playful cherubs, surrounded by gilded scrolls, painted over the doors. There are several simple wooden neoclassical-style chairs with matte, old white paint that has gently distressed over time. To bring more light and shiny, glistening splendor to the room, to contrast with the matte paintwork and washed floorboards, there are several mirrors, some etched with a mirrored candle sconce, a central glistening crystal chandelier, and matching wall sconces. The room is on the corner of the house, so light streams in from two directions through tall windows.

[above, left] The design of this chair is typical of the neoclassical style that was prevalent in Sweden. The column-like legs draw more inspiration from architecture than any other style of furniture design.

[left] Gold leaf of this period has quite a different appearance from later examples, up to the present day. It was quite a warm, coppery color, with not as much of a yellow glow. This allows it to work very well with its red-oxide paint backing, which can be seen where the leaf has worn away.

[opposite] The soft, matte texture of the off-white walls works in beautiful contrast to the glitz and shine of the chandelier and gilded panel borders in this drawing room.

[overleaf, left] Curvaceous, long-case Mora clocks, such as this one, first appeared in the rococo period, and they have become perhaps the most iconic design of the Gustavian period.

[overleaf, right] The painting built into the panel in the over-lintel is from China. Although the pink color on these walls is common in Swedish design, the combination with green is unusual. It works because the two colors complement each other, and it suits the room by picking up on colors in the Chinese painting.

The idea of combining a light green and pink may not seem initially to be a sound one, but actually the colors are very complementary. It's a great combination and it works very well. The pink can be created using Antoinette or Scandinavian Pink with Old White; the green is made from Antibes with some white and a little Aubusson Blue.

Another similarly lightly colored room is a boudoir, where exquisite, hand-painted Chinese wallpaper lines the walls. The intricate detailing and sensitive hand-painting were not immediately apparent to us, but as we looked, we became entranced with the delicately painted flowers, buds, and tiny leaves trailing, with just a hint of the paper's Chinese heritage. It is painted in deep blue washes with an inky blue-black outline and highlights of white. What we loved most was that nothing was wasted and it's not perfectly aligned, with an almost random, patchwork approach. Instead of strips being laid rigidly from the ceiling, if, for instance, a particularly fine butterfly was in danger of being cut off, it was merely cut around. This wallpaper was executed almost 300 years ago in China and imported—we could only wonder at how exotic it must have seemed when it arrived in the house.

[overleaf] Entering this room brought a smile to our faces. The wall paintings are unsophisticated, almost naïve, but are very pleasing, depicting farming scenes, hunting, hay making, and dancing. The color palette is in fact quite limited, comprising a gray-blue landscape (Paris Grey and Aubusson Blue) and figures in warm, earthy reds (Primer Red and Scandinavian Pink).

PRINT **ROOM**

One of the most charming rooms in the house is the dining room. We found it was full of humor and creativity—we could imagine the family gathering pictures and working on the display together.

Part of the charm is the unfinished feel, as the prints were not glued to the wall but merely tacked on. The collection of etchings is like a scrapbook of favorite images arranged symmetrically, tacked in place with a border painted around each, complete with a painted hook and thread. A few have a real frame around them. Any theme was lost on us, but maybe they depict favorite places, stories, and heroes.

This style is based on the idea of a Print Room, a popular craft, particularly in the 18th century, which was often undertaken by the women in the house. (There is a particularly fine example in Castletown House in Ireland, done by Lady Louisa Conolly.)

The room in Stola, of course, largely uses paint instead of printed borders and frames. The colors are earth pigments—yellow ocher and green earth. They were probably available locally, and mixed using a binder either of animal glue or perhaps milk or egg yolk, products that were all widely available in a farming area like Stola.

[opposite, above] Although impressive, the craftsmanship here is very simple. We found it so inspiring because it's the sort of thing that anyone could easily do at home. The whole thing is based around using different shades of just two colors, a wash on the wall, and loose brushwork. Prints can easily be found in old books or secondhand stores.

[above] The freehand painting on the walls of this room are almost like a caricature of a neoclassical print room. The picture frames have been painted directly on the wall with painterly flair. The composition of the frames, however, has the symmetrical precision of neoclassical design.

My take on the loosely painted border, which is based on a classical design, is cheerfully uneven and playful, over a gentle, mottled wash of the same green-gray with Old White.

paint your own

Marble effect

Many years ago, looking at Swedish country furniture, I was inspired by this marble effect. It is more like a pattern based on the look of marble, rather than an accurate representation. When we saw this door by the staircase, I was excited and delighted, as only a few weeks before I'd been doing a table in a frottage technique to try to achieve a similar look. I have tried this technique in several ways, with a paint and glaze mix, with a watery paint on paint, and, finally, with watery paint over waxed paint. I have found the final technique is best, especially on furniture.

The effect is achieved by applying a layer of paint and leaving it to dry. Prepare a load of newspaper sheets, crumpled up and then laid out flat. Next, apply a layer of wax to the paintwork and then make a watery mix of water and paint. Test it by applying the paint to the surface and seeing if it is translucent. If the brushmark you make is too opaque, add more water.

Paint an area slightly larger than a sheet of the newspaper and immediately lay the sheet down and rub it flat with your hands, so the excess liquid comes off onto the paper. Work quickly to remove the paper. You should have a broken paintwork look caused by the crumpled paper and the wet paint being absorbed unevenly. On my table, I did a flat base of Scandinavian Pink, a layer of wax, a layer of frottaged Cream, a layer of wax, and then a layer of frottaged Aubusson Blue, finishing with a layer of wax.

[opposite] This door is one of the oldest in Stola and predates the 18th-century modernization. It is probably more than 300 years old.

[left] Greek Blue, Barcelona Orange, with a little Aubusson Blue to adjust the colors, plus cream, can be combined to produce this marble effect.

Chapter 3

modern retro

We find the bold and fresh-faced designs of modern retro inspired and inspiring. It is all about doing things in a new way, and looking to the future.

This innovative style emerged in the postwar years with a switch from drab black and white to modern, modular, and technicolor. It was the era of the "new look"—and what a look it was, especially the colors, patterns, and graphics. A new streamlined aesthetic, along with new materials in furniture and decor, saw the arrival of wonderfully curved, contoured, and spiral shapes. Anything was possible with the new technologies, and this "future" style avoided, at all costs, referencing "old-fashioned" prewar designs.

Modern retro references the atomic age, the space race, new plastics, pharmaceuticals, and polyester (to name a few modern innovations). Postwar design was all about the "new look" in art, architecture, transport, fashion, and graphics. New modular, cellular, and rounded shapes were made possible by the innovation and mass production of plastics, glass, and laminates. Molded plywood furniture with compound curves and fluid shapes was available for the first time, and functional living became the new buzzword.

[opposite] An open-plan, decluttered, Finnish interior crafted in natural materials. The centerpiece is the deeply recessed modern white fiberglass Karuselli lounge chair, designed by Yrjö Kukkapuro for Avarte in 1964. The chrome and light brown leather chairs were designed by Marcel Breuer in 1925.

[above] An original "modern" glass-topped, steel-framed 1950s sideboard. It shows bold contrasts with its black enameled metal frame against strong yellow drawers.

elements of **Modern Retro** style

Patterns

For a style that has a "sparse" and streamlined aesthetic, modern retro still allows room for a highly decorative approach in its textiles, kitchenware, and furnishings. In fact, we feel it is as much defined by the futuristic and funky patterns on its ceramics, wallpapers, and textiles as by its functionality and modular approach to interiors and furniture design.

Fueled by the race into outer space and the inner space of the atom, Americans, especially, embraced everything atomic. The atom became a key design motif in the 1950s and 1960s. Squares and circles, rounded squares, rocket-shaped cones, and other new space-age motifs were also typical at this time.

Abstract art is when artists draw out the form, color, and line of objects to represent them differently. It was the other key influence on modern retro patterns, typography, and designs. For example, it was not about painting a rose or palm tree naturally; it was about abstracting it to make it almost like a pattern—simplifying it as much as possible into single lines and shapes and then repeating the motif in a completely synthesized way. We find this mix of science and art really refreshing, and the patterns produced in this period incredibly exciting and eye-catching.

Essentially with modern retro, science became sexy and the backdrop for exciting designs and patterns in clothes and in the home. Nowhere was this more clearly evident than at the 1951 Festival of Britain. This postwar showcase for all things modern featured, for example, textile designs with patterns inspired by x-ray crystallography (the arrangement of atoms). Terence Conran began his 50 years as a designer at the festival, and also started out by creating textile designs based on similar swirling microscopic imagery. Modern microscopes were revealing a new world of cellular structures, and this was very much brought into designs.

Three variations on the modern retro style, both in shape and the combinations of colors and patterns. These designs derive from the idea of fruit cut open with seeds and sections removed. The image was simplified and made a little abstract, while the colors were based around primary and secondary colors with blacks and grays.

Sinewy, fluid, and organic lines, as seen under a microscope, were hand-drawn into new abstract patterns on tableware and soft furnishings. Instead of a leaf as a design, for example, you had the leaf's structure as revealed under the microscope, further abstracted with lots of swirls and modular shapes and then highly colorized.

[opposite] The 16-square grid, as seen on these retro cushions, was a popular framework to showcase abstract doodles next to full-color squares. They are piled onto the archetypal modular stacking chair created by hugely influential Danish designer Arne Jacobsen in the 1950s.

[above] This ceramic tile panel by Lubna Chowdhary shows pop art-inspired circles in a black rectangular frame. It complements the grid-like, thick black lines of the poster above, by Anki Josefsson and Anneli Sandström of One Must Dash. The funky turquoise pottery sits on a cabinet painted in colors inspired by cubist and expressionist artist Paul Klee.

[right] These plates and tray are good examples of modern retro patterns. The linear, abstract designs, acid colors, swirling, squiggly lines, and grid squares reference Paul Klee's 1950s retro abstract expressionist doodles. Other popular patterns included roulette curves (such as those created by the Spirograph drawing toy) and abacus-like collections of simplified geometric shapes, as well as natural forms such as stones and shells.

Shape

In this new postwar era, instead of interiors being adorned with decorative elements and ornate flourishes of the past, it was the shape of the furniture that was decorative in itself. Modern retro saw space-age motifs combined with a streamlined, functional design to produce an amazing and original array of furniture and furnishings. Modern materials and construction methods came to the fore, along with a new breed of designers to shape them. Sleek, streamlined, and molded shapes in wood, plastics, and other new man-made materials became fashionable, especially with Danish designers. Low coffee tables, minimalist side tables, wood-framed sofas, wall fixtures, and freestanding cabinets, designed to hold a record player as well as drinks, became all the rage.

New molding processes allowed for contoured and sculptural shapes to be manufactured in man-made plywood (thin sheets of wood veneer) such as MDF (medium-density fiberboard) and chipboard (made of particles). Starburst clocks and mirrors, kidney-shaped tables (like an artist's palette), and even boomerang shapes were now available in home furnishings. Accessories were no longer "square" (both in look and in the emotive language of the 1960s). Other modern materials such as plastic binding, and bent steel legs on rubber shock mounts completed the space-age designs. Husband and wife designers Charles and Ray Eames were at the forefront of this new, bold, modern design in the U.S. These new interiors were perfectly suited to the open-plan bungalows and stylish, compact apartments people were beginning to live in.

While it appears there is an "anything goes" feel to retro, you do need to choose carefully. You may go for the "far out" plastic shapes of the 1960s, such as a boomerang-shaped, orange fiberglass desk, but there's a fine line between cool retro and kitsch. Ultimately, it comes down to personal taste, but other factors to consider when choosing furniture are the shape and size of your room, the shapes of the items already there, and your color scheme. Visiting design museums and exhibitions will give you some pointers. Also, look online at design companies like G Plan, Ercol, and Knoll, and the works of designers such as Arne Jacobson, Eero Saarinen, Charles and Ray Eames, George Nelson, and Gio Ponti, to name a few. Danish designer Arne Jacobsen, for example, produced the Series 7 modular chair (see page 62) in 1955, and it remains to this day pretty much the blueprint for all modular laminated stacking chairs. It is the most popular chair ever designed, with over five million made. Its success is down to its shape and functionality—he designed it to save space and to be portable for people who were now eating in kitchen/dining areas.

[opposite, above] This sideboard, displaying some retro pieces, is a clean-cut, eye-catching storage piece for decluttering a living space. The shapely armchair, positioned beside a modern reading lamp, has been upholstered in a stylish blue tweed. The side tables are kidney-shaped, retro-style reproductions. The screen is from a modern furniture store.

[opposite, below] A pure retro side cabinet with its matte steel ballerina legs and simple, stripped-back rectilinear shape. The curvy, yellow pottery and oil and vinegar jars, with the abstract wooden trunk wallpaper behind, complete this fine ensemble.

[above, left] The sunburst concave mirror is one of several nonlinear shapes along this wall. The wallflower-style lamp above the reading chair is a quirky but eye-catching fixture.

[above, center] Vibrantly colored, hand-blown glass vases and decanters are popular modern retro items.

[above, right] The injection-molded plastic S chair by Danish designer Verner Panton in the 1960s is as space-age as they come. It was the first single-component plastic chair and was produced in a range of primary colors, including this glossy fire-engine red.

The patterns of the time reflect the inspiration of abstract painters such as the Spanish artist Joan Miró, as well as from science and natural forms. Circles, blobs, spirals, and angled lines with cube shapes and rectangles were often done in secondary colors and were a standard decoration.

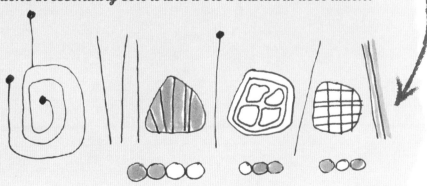

[left] This metal-frame, 1950s furniture is vigorously streamlined. The shape of the futuristic clock references designer George Nelson's Atom Ball Clock, inspired by atomic power and the space race—a very modern retro theme.

Colors

The explosion in colors that the modern retro style brought was not unlike the difference between watching color television after only ever seeing black and white. The colorful painted furniture, glass, ceramics, textiles, and interiors mirrored the myriad new shapes in furniture and accessories. Advances in science made possible a new range of brighter, bolder synthetic colors that could be mass-produced. More paint colors became available than ever before, and colored plastic particularly summed up the new look. The potential of color in plastics was not lost on the new wave of designers, who saw it as a way of getting people out of their "beige" comfort zone, encouraging them to have real color in the house for the first time.

We believe color is a fantastic way to spark people's imagination and so, too, did the groundbreaking designers such as Charles and Ray Eames, Verner Panton, and Arne Jacobsen. Primary colors and ameba-shaped forms seem so right for each other now but it was a bold move back in the 1950s and 1960s. Bright orange and red bowls, lime green lamp stands, yellow fiberglass stacking chairs, upholstered chairs and Formica tables, pale blue kitchen cabinets, deep blue wine glasses—these are all modern retro in terms of color and were so exciting compared to what had gone before. In contrast to all these bright primaries, black was used as a cool neutral.

[left] A modern retro coat rack displaying atomic particles in the shape of multicolored knobs. The yellows and oranges complement the predominantly black metal, sculptural coat stand.

My illustration shows the simplified abstract leaf shape that was ubiquitous in the 1950s and 60s and appeared in a myriad of designs. It was used on fabrics, plates, cups, and kitchen items. The colors were bright in the 1950s, but toward the 1960s, they became more neutral, with browns, oranges, and sage greens. A textured fabric called barkcloth was often used at this time.

  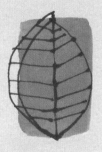   

The Scandinavian designers working with real wood tended to use restrained designs and muted colors to emphasize the natural grain and tone of the wood, which was mostly teak. The color palette became much more brash and gaudy in the 1960s and 1970s, referencing the pop art of Roy Lichtenstein and Andy Warhol.

Color really comes into its own when used on ceramics and textiles. For the first time, buyers could mix and match kitchen and dining services from a palette of complementary colors. It was the opposite of the Model T Ford maxim, "You can paint it any color, so long as it's black." Designers took an uninhibited approach to color, not just in color-drenched furniture but also in flamboyant soft furnishings and upholstery fabrics. It was the use of loud colors that helped simplify natural shapes into abstract patterns so typical of modern retro designs.

[above] The 1960s brought flowers into interiors again, used by designers such as Mary Quant. These tiles show the bright, basic colors inspired by the then new colored plastics and the simple stylized patterns.

[right] A beautifully colored and proportioned chest of drawers, in two units that can close on a vertical hinge. The drawers are in gradated shades of blue and orange, yellow and red, and mimic the abstract art of Gino Severini, who fused cubism with futurism.

[below] My illlustration of a cabinet showing how you might try your own gradated color scheme. From the top, it features Provence, Barcelona Orange, Greek Blue, and Graphite. See also page 78 for a Paul Klee-inspired piece.

a retro London home

This fabulous 1960s house exudes style and sophistication. Designer Virginia Armstrong has cleverly combined 1950s and 1960s pieces with her own and other modern designers' work to create a very stylish home filled with life and light.

Using her design skills, Virgina has evolved a sophisticated take on modern retro. She has been inspired, in particular, by Scandinavian style, and by pieces from the Netherlands, Russia, and Britain, with a nod to European folk art too. The feel is 1950s–60s, and the interiors are fully functioning and perfectly in keeping with the architecture.

This five-floor house is one of a row set on a hillside. The panoramic views over London are revealed through the large picture windows, which also give a spacious and airy feeling.

If you love a Victorian villa or a quaint country cottage, a 1960s modular-looking home may appear to offer little in the way of cozy comfort. But we loved the simple lines and shapes and color palette. Based on squares and rectangles, there are no unnecessary decorative details to soften the look. White walls predominate and there is a cool color scheme throughout. Virginia's basic message is lots of light, limited color, and clear, organic, simple shapes— and it works brilliantly.

COOL, CLEAN, AND AIRY

The open-plan living room with a dining area and kitchen has one wall almost completely filled with a large floor-to-ceiling window, and this is what you see as you enter the house. The panoramic window is a key design feature of the period. Not being overlooked means there is no need for curtains, so not a bit of light is lost.

White—a clean, bright but soft white—is the wash of color that greets you. This is counterpointed by a very limited palette, mainly yellowed-green with a blued-gray, and pine-colored wood. There are also very few and quite small areas of orange. So, the room is essentially cool colors with a little "hot" orange to catch the eye and set the whole space alight.

Mixing contemporary, vintage, and traditional pieces is part of the great success of this room, as it does not slavishly keep to the 1960s but includes an old gilded mirror and contemporary cushions.

[previous page] In the dining area there are several classic mid-century furniture designs. The drop-shaped table and chair bases are typical of the molded plastic style pioneered by Eero Saarinen in 1956, when he designed the Tulip chair. Molded plastic was an exciting new technology in the 1950s and 1960s (see page 64).

[below] The Ercol daybed, a classic British design by Lucian Ercolani, has rounded edges echoing the shapes of the molded plastic furniture. This model mid-century piece does not look at all out of place with a mix of classic and contemporary cushions designed by Virginia herself and the influential British designer Lucienne Day. The black and white flower cushion on the right is by Heather Moore of Skinny laMinx.

[opposite, below left] Another ergonomically designed chair, this time in vinyl wicker with modular metal legs. The design was called satellite (echoing a satellite dish and the public's preoccupation with the space race). The cushion patterns echo the grid-with-simple-shapes look that was so prevalent in textile designs of the time.

[opposite, below right] Displaying books front on brings life to shelves. The covers of these books, published in the early 1960s, really set a period scene.

A laminated world map is the retro design for the seat and support on a 1950s school chair. If you are confident, you could try customizing something like this yourself.

Including the kitchen as a dining or serving area in living spaces was a fairly new concept for the public in the 1960s. In this house, the kitchen was originally a separate room but the wall was knocked down to make it open-plan.

Open shelving with simple-shaped bowls and functional pans are displayed in a decorative way. They are kept tidy and neat by keeping color to a minimum. Any color in the room comes from the materials—wood, marble, clay pottery, plastics, and iron, looking clean and smart against the gray wall.

[left] Oil and vinegar jars became fashionable and more common in London in the 1960s, as did various plastic serving spoons and forks. The new plastic molding technology allowed for futuristic, flowing, ergonomic shapes.

[above] This kitchen has been made to look so typical of the modern retro style by bringing together a great collection of retro ceramics alongside some modern touches. The metal electric kettle, the Holkham, Midwinter, and Hornsea ceramics, and even the inclusion of a pineapple put this kitchen firmly in its period. The white geometric light fitting by Studio Snowpuppe gives the room a contemporary anchor.

[opposite] This coffee pot and teapot are both typically 1960s, with their simple cylindrical shapes and clean look. The tray is a modern take on a 1960s textile design by the home's owner, Virginia Armstrong. She has used simplified shapes, abstracted from natural imagery (tree trunks and tree rings), which were typical of mid-century pattern design.

SIMPLE AND **STYLISH**

Upstairs, above the kitchen and dining room, is one large room with a balcony and a huge panoramic window. This is the living room, where there are sofas, chairs, a sideboard, and a working fireplace. As you enter the room, the fireplace is on the left with the sideboard facing. The sofas and chairs around the fire make a great focal point. With other forms of heating being available, 1960s houses often had no fireplace but where there is one, as here, it is often very simple or made from natural materials such as stone and wood. A mantelpiece would have been considered a superfluous decorative embellishment for a streamlined Scandinavian house. The logs of silver birch add a light touch to the Scandinavian influence.

Scandinavian design made a huge impact on homes all over the world from the 1950s onward, as they developed a design idea where beautiful and functional everyday objects should be affordable for everyone. Furniture was made light and often from teak, rather than the heavy ornate and dark pieces common before World War II. The long, low sideboard, often with sliding doors and smooth recessed handles in a light-colored wood, became an important statement piece in any contemporary room.

[previous spread] Sideboards, especially "G-Plan," are quintessential modern retro pieces. Displayed on this one there is a collection of ceramics, book covers, and glassware along with a Swiss cheese plant, popular at the time, as it had such great strong shape. The modular 1960s Ladderax shelving unit above brings some height to the arrangement.

[opposite] A beautiful example of atomic-era design is this mirror, the sunburst rays reminiscent of the structure of an atom. Yet the shape simultaneously echoes the chrysanthemum print on the right—a design by Tretchikoff, more famously known for *The Chinese Girl*, a ubiquitous image in the '60s. The old school chair has been made into a personal period piece—it is decoupaged with a vintage map of the local area.

[above] So much about mid-century design emulated simplified natural forms and imagery. These shelves are modern but in keeping with this aesthetic. The real wooden branches have been painted white, for a neat, simple look. The shelves house a personal collection of objects that draw on mid-century Scandinavian design but not slavishly. The collection is brought together by the selective color palette and bird theme.

Complementary colors

Find a piece of furniture where there is no strut between the drawers, so the colors can flow seamlessly from one to the other. There are many variations to these chest of drawers, some with integrated recessed handles and others with handles. I chose to paint the outer casing in Graphite, which works with the modern print on the wall and against the white wall, so it is delineated, but you could try using Original or Pure instead, or at least a neutral or other dark color.

Apart from the outer color, just two colors are used here, and to work well they must be two complementaries. I chose Barcelona Orange and Greek Blue but you could use any two, as long as they are at opposite ends of the color wheel (see pages 218–219).

I took out all the drawers (remember the order) and started by painting the bottom one Greek Blue. I used a roller tray for the paint, so I could add Barcelona Orange until I liked the color, and then painted the next drawer. I added a little more of the Barcelona Orange each time until I liked the color and it was sufficiently different from the previous one. I carried on until I had one drawer left and then painted this with Barcelona Orange. You could, of course, measure each color and make the development more mathematical.

This piece was inspired by the Swiss artist Paul Klee, from a small painting he did in 1922. Klee was one of the Bauhaus painters, a design school that hugely influenced postwar design and, not least, my approach to painting.

[top] This small cabinet is painted in Olive, with the legs painted in Paloma, a light gray. Neutral grays are very modern retro. The inside drawer of this small cabinet is an Annie Sloan stencil created using Pure on Aubusson Blue.

[above] This swatch features the colors used on the drawers—Barcelona Orange and Greek Blue—and shows how they mix to make a grayish-green in the middle.

Chapter 4

bohemian

We're big fans of bohemian or "boho." This arty style has lots of brio—clashing colors, patterns, and cultures are somehow all pulled together to look fabulous. The knack for today's boho devotee is how to give the style a coherent feel, without it looking muddled and "messy."

The bohemian home has its heart in Paris in the 1920s, when artists, writers, actors, and musicians of the "Jazz Age" were drawn to the French capital. Many were flamboyant and uninhibited by social constraints or morals. They lived frugally in shabby studios and attics, in gypsy neighborhoods, stuffed with decorative bits and pieces they collected as decor and as "set designs" for their paintings. These artists adopted and adapted the exotic, folksy, and freewheeling lifestyle of the local gypsies, who were believed to have come from Bohemia, and the name stuck. As artists ourselves, we feel a natural affinity to this "having no boundaries" approach.

I have been influenced by Charleston's vibrant interiors—the early 20th-century English country retreat of the Bloomsbury Group. A worldwide vocabulary of patterns, colors, designs, and textures is there for the taking, often with a touch of the surreal and the absurd.

[opposite] The random elements of this bedroom—the wild flowers, the oil painting, the bright, expressionist floral bedspread, and the raw, unpainted wooden headboard—are unified by the strong graphite wall color. So what makes it boho? Well, one pointer is the portrait randomly resting on the headboard, rather than hanging on the wall, framed, which would be the conventional approach.

[above] In this cabinet there is a seeming clash of religious works. An Ancient Egyptian cat god and an ancient bronze of a finely detailed Indian god are displayed with a brightly colored porcelain statuette of Mary and baby Jesus.

elements of bohemian style

Clashing patterns

The whole point of bohemian is that patterns should be mixed together —and liberties taken. That is fundamental to this style. So why not run together, for example, tartan with paisley patterns, paisley with flowers, or circular patterns with zigzags? To do this without one pattern being negated, there has to be something to bring them all together. This is usually a common color, or an item such as a trim, that can bring a unifying theme. When using lots of patterns and colors in a bold and harmonizing way, it can help to have a dark color, such as graphite, as a backdrop.

The sources for the patterns, such as the cultural references, should be deliberately diverse, from across the globe and from different centuries. Old World, New World, modern, or ancient, the source, shapes, and sizes are up to you. However, try to keeping a unifying color or design. In the room shown on the opposite page, for example, highly varied patterns work because the color palette harmonizes them and they are set against a backdrop of a single-color painted wall.

Getting it right is not easy, and your first combinations might look messy and a muddle. You may need to experiment to find the links that bring everything together, perhaps trying out more patterns with similar shapes, or more patterns that come with complementary background colors.

The array of different-shaped and patterned cushions and pillows works well here because they share a white or off-white background.

[opposite] The bed has an amazing overlay of differing patterned covers and throws. The Indian multipatterned cushions are also as apparently random as the covers, while the floral carpet and bedside cabinet appear to add to the clash. What unifies these patterns is the color scheme, which is predominantly warm pinks and purples, with black and white, and the patterns, which are mainly made with circular shapes and floral motifs.

[above, right] The open book, glass, paintings, and vase of flowers on the piano combine vintage finds with ethnically diverse references.

Clashing cultures

The most important element of bohemian style is the clashing of cultures—the juxtaposition of differing cultural decorative elements. The other styles in this book tend to have one single dominant cultural theme. Neoclassical is a good example, with its overarching stylized form. But with bohemian, you might turn neoclassical on its head, literally. You could take a classic Greek bust and paint it orange, thereby transforming it. You are now using it in a surreal way, yet taking care that it works alongside other cultural elements. You have gone bohemian!

Surrealism has influenced this style. A knowledge of art and culture is not essential but it does help to have a sense of the absurd. It's about taking an educated guess and being confident. You might, for example, feel sufficiently playful to put a vintage flapper's cloche hat on a bust of Napoleon. All "bohemians" will have their own sense of the absurd and surreal. Felix has a really nice pair of pliers on his mantelpiece because he likes them, and it is a little bit absurd. The Bloomsbury Group painted and installed an amazing variety of cultural references and artifacts in their country retreat at Charleston, for example, but kept the whole vision unified by using a very painterly effect of subdued colors in all the interiors.

Bohemian style is open to many interpretations and difficult to get right. You source your decor from worldwide cultures, civilizations, and possibly religions (and that could be a statement about your beliefs or just what you find attractive), and from primitive tribal art to pop art or surrealism. Your choices may be eclectic but the trick is to harmonize them by placing them with sympathetically colored and patterned furniture, pieces, and decor.

In the room interiors shown here, you can see that bohemian is as much a lifestyle choice as a style. These rooms are about deconstructing, and then making a statement. They reference the idea of the artist's studio where collections of interesting objects are placed, perhaps to be painted later as still-life portraits.

[above] A collection of objects that might be found in an artist's studio makes for an intriguing room interior. A dummy's head, dried flowers, a Turkish bust on its plinth, a vase of poppies, and so on. Such a mix may seem weird but it is boho, especially with the books and magazines on display.

[below] A border I drew taking inspiration from a wide variety of sources. There's some Indian paisley, a goose from folk art design, and some Aztec influence too. It has all been done as a doodle, and the joy is that anything can be added.

There is an apparent Nordic theme on this concrete wall but look closer and you'll discover a henna glove. The effect works visually, both in the careful arrangement and the natural rawness of the display. It is clashing cultures—a really striking and inquisitive mash-up of decor.

[above] The "ART" letters, leftovers from an old store sign, were picked and painted by Felix to go on top of this old wood-grained cabinet that I had bought. I love the result.

[left] The display takes on a sophisticated scrapbook approach, which includes a gun, children's drawings, drawings of children, a framed skull and skeleton, industrial cogs, and tribal masks. The dominant black shelf is mounted at the same low level as a pile of Turkish floor cushions, which together neatly underscore the whole ensemble.

Clashing colors

So what are clashing colors? They are two, mainly secondary and tertiary, colors that sit in a similar part of the color wheel (see pages 218–219) but that are separated by a color. Red and purple, for instance, sit in the warm part of the color wheel and are separated by deep crimson/burgundy red. Used well, these colors look stunning together.

Bright purplish-pink and orange (a pink made by mixing Emperor's Silk with Pure and then Barcelona Orange) is a great "hot" example of clashing colors, and we've used it to great effect on several projects. Other clashing combinations might include turquoise and lemon-lime, turquoise and purple, bluish-emerald green and turquoise. Using clashing colors does not mean that a riot of color and pattern is essential—the painting can be restrained and still eye-catching.

My paint colors are based on the artist's palette approach, rather than the color chart approach. What this means is that the color range is deliberately limited, but actually you get endless color variation possibilities from that palette because the pigments are designed to be mixed. My paints give you more creative freedom, which is tailor-made for bohemian style.

Sometimes the clashing colors can look slightly uncomfortable together, so you need to be careful when combining a lot of bright colors. If you start with purple and bright pinky-red, or go with the blues and greens, you will find these easy to clash because there's so much color variation in between.

[above, left] The wall map of Scandinavia with its strong blues, orange, and yellow works really well beside the greeny-turquoise study desk. Yellowy-green to bluey-green can often look terrible together but here, with the brown tabletop and pencil holders, the colors, although not a conventional match, look lively and eye-catching.

[above, right] The textured, red velvet Victorian throw sits well in front of the kitsch, 1950s, predominantly orange and blue, Las Vegas scene.

[above] You can use an awful lot of different colors if you include black, graphite, or white (Old White). Using graphite makes the whole mix more edgy.

Here are some slightly unusual combinations. Top: Antoinette, Barcelona Orange, and a pink made from mixing Pure with Emperor's Silk. Middle: Antibes Green with English Yellow, Old Violet, and Scandinavian Pink. Bottom: Arles, Provence, and Burgundy.

My illustration of Russian nesting dolls suggest color combinations that work well in a bohemian interior.

boho cottage

We were met with an incredible explosion of color when we visited Janice Issitt's spectacular house in the heart of the English countryside. She likens her characterful home to a moving target, which she is constantly changing. Janice wanted it to be "in keeping" with her surroundings and she has succeeded. It is not at all apparent that you are in a 1980s house, sitting between a 16th-century thatch cottage and an 1890s Victorian dwelling. She has transformed her home into a very stylish house, bursting with beautiful boho features.

Janice loves collecting objects and has a "why-have-one-when-you-can-have-20" approach. She inherited this from her father, who had a large collections of clocks, watches, fruit knives, and other bits and pieces. Janice is a photographer and she likes to set "scenes," with the idea that different sections of the house look like a set design. This is her springboard for going bohemian—taking groups of objects and making more sense of them visually as an ensemble than as individual objects.

Look at the part of her living room shown opposite. The mirror, painted white to draw it out, is an English Victorian overmantel, but it makes a great wall feature. The mix of cultural influences is clearly evident: the Austrian vintage cuckoo clock, the Indian cushions and throw, the Russian nesting doll, all beneath a French chandelier—it is a clash of cultures held together by the deep Florence.

The living room is the epitome of Janice's bohemian style. There is an English cottage feel to it, brought out especially by the brightly colored floor mat, the collection of Victorian flower paintings, and the embroidered bits and pieces. But then you see the folk influences, particularly Russian, Scandinavian, and the Indian table, pouf, and throw. Add to this the "otherworldly" influences, such as the Catholic statuettes and 1960s English ceramics, and you can tell that Janice has a curator's eye for detail and what works together.

Janice shares her home with her partner Ian Roberts, a composer and musician. She herself was in the music business, and on her travels overseas developed a keen eye for the quirky, the exotic, and the cultural "rock'n'roll" decor.

But this room is not just a collection of different objects; it is about the sum of the parts. Janice has added the reclaimed pine floor, the cast-iron Victorian fireplace, and the shutters to give the room character. She found the fireplace on eBay, and she and Ian put down the reclaimed pine floorboards—the actual floor is concrete.

A VISUAL POTPOURRI

[previous page] One end of Janice's long living room shows her display of seemingly clashing cultural objects, including a 1950s Austrian cuckoo clock, a lampshade made from a Russian head scarf, a painted Victorian mantel with painted candles, and Indian throws and cushions. The ensemble is held together tightly by the strong Florence painted wall.

[opposite] Looking down the living room, you can see Janice's style is not just bohemian—there's also a mix of vintage floral and modern retro. As Janice shows, it is okay to mix styles; you don't have to follow one single style exclusively.

[above] A well-considered layout for a gallery of mostly Victorian floral imagery (but including a 1960s Peter Blake painting) with some embroidered works, also framed—perfect for a white wall.

As soon as we entered the living room, we knew it had been done very well. It is a long room displaying its cultural, color, and pattern influences up and down the natural wood floor. It's also very light with strong colors at either end: Aubusson Blue on the wall at one end, with Florence and Old White at the other. People are often scared to use such strong colors, but if you use them with a lot of white or Old White around them—and pick up those colors with individual decorative items—they look colorful without being overpowering or overwhelming.

VIBRANT COLORS

Going upstairs, the central landing has little natural light but Janice has done it up extremely well by painting the walls with Barcelona Orange, and then adding a multipatterned, floral Indian chest of drawers in various shades of blue with yellow framing.

This furniture piece is new, from a wholesale Indian furniture and giftware supplier. Janice was so drawn to it because it packs a punch and she believed, rightly as it happens, that hallways and landings like hers can take the vibrancy of the Barcelona Orange wall.

A print of Peter Blake's *Babe Rainbow* (the original was made in 1968) hangs above this chest. Janice has several pieces by the 1960s pop

[above, left] No clashing colors but a mix of cultures (perhaps in a playful way) in this alcove displaying figures of Jesus and of Mary with baby Jesus, next to an Indian turquoise container and a traditional English mantelpiece clock. All the decor here is framed in off-white colors. Above the display is a stencil by Janice of birds in an Eastern European folk-art motif. The recessed cabinet is MDF but the fretwork and Old White distressed paintwork have given it added texture and interest.

[left] This chair was covered by Janice using an antique suzani (a traditional embroidered textile from Uzbekistan), which she bought some time ago. She was given the chair but did not like the fabric on it, so she reupholstered it with this native folk art. The flowers in the bright turquoise vase work very well here too.

[opposite] Janice's eye for the visually vibrant shows in these 1960s West German vases, sometimes called "Lava" ceramics because the glaze flows down like volcanic lava. She collected them before they were collectibles. The candles in this folky Scandinavian holder (it's not a menora, although it looks like one) are hand-painted, so they are very much for decorative effect. The real flowers are arum lilies and anemones.

artist, although she points out she's not in the earnings bracket for a total original. Her *Babe Rainbow*, however, is an original 1968 lithoprint on tin. She tracked this fictitious lady wrestler down after some research. Janice's art knowledge is a key factor in giving her the confidence to go boho.

Janice was also sent a Peter Blake limited-edition signed print by his wife after Janice had made some things for the family. It is in the gold frame with the collection of other art in the lounge, and is the larger one with flowers growing up a wall. There are other pieces around the house, all signed and limited, including *Liberty Blake in a Kimono* and *The Owl and the Pussycat.*

Along the way to the bathroom we pass the dining hallway with amazing shutters at the windows. Janice found it almost impossible to find old shutters to fit her windows, so she went for a maximum and minimum size and treated it more like wall styling. The shutters are too long for the window but they create the effect that the window is much larger than it actually is. This area of the house is quite dark and, originally, curtains restricted the light, but now the shutters seem to refract the light around. Janice has kept them exactly as they came out of an old barn, before they were stored in a salvage yard for years.

[above] Detail of the Indian cupboard revealing in detail the delicate, abstract, multicolored floral designs against vibrant blues and yellows.

[above] The bright orange metal pitcher sits well alongside the Barcelona Orange wall and folk-inspired Indian mug.

Clashing imagery and culture are held in check by the just-as-lively Barcelona Orange painted wall, and the yellow stripes found on both the modern Indian cupboard and the Peter Blake "Babe Rainbow" print above it. The clash of patterns is also evident here, with the smooth, linear, colored surrounds of the pop-art print and the floral marquetry of the cupboard.

The pink basin of a vintage enamel French lavabo makes a bold color choice against the wooden, turquoise, wall-mounted pedestal on which it sits. The rolled small towels add yet more vibrant colors.

BOHO BATHROOM

On entering the bathroom, we both looked at each other and said, "Wow!" It is simply stunning—a very bold treatment for a bathroom. If there is a predominant theme here, I suppose it veers on the bohemian "gypsy." The green patterned Indian sari acting as a curtain reinforces that look.

This striking room shows a great use of color and that's what we particularly liked about it. This is not your typical bathroom; Janice has designed it in an unconventional way. She is not saying, "It's a bathroom, so it has to be blue." She's deconstructed it, eliminated the obvious coastal artifacts, and used a startlingly and unexpected main theme, which simply doesn't fall into the usual clichés. The pink (which is a Henrietta mix) is certainly an unusual bathroom color but it works really well, especially as it is offset against the Florence of the freestanding rolltop bathtub and the wall cabinet. The cabinet was originally off-white and is part of, and supports, the 1900s pink French water dispenser for washing hands—called a lavabo—which is in its original color. This vintage item provided the inspiration for the wall color.

The color combination has a deliberate Indian feel. The cultures on display here include English Victorian, French turn-of-the-century, and contemporary Indian. The gilded feet of the bathtub are particularly

[opposite] A pink and white Victorian wash pitcher reinforces the color and cultural style of this bathroom. The Indian sari, acting as a curtain, comes from a completely different culture. There is a mixture of styles, with the driftwood wall hanging (more coastal than chic) with two Indian birds, and the swan vase with ferns. The decor is not really even about being a bathroom, which is exciting.

[above] The French enamel lavabo is used decoratively rather than functionally. It is the sort of washing setup popular in many French country homes in the "Jazz Age."

eye-catching and, again, unexpected in the color mix. Janice has used the space well (in fact, she told me she had to knock a wall down to make the bathroom bigger) but, ultimately, it is the unconventional color mix that brings it all together.

Another upstairs room took us to the spare bedroom, which is really spectacular. The wall is painted in my Provence and Antibes Green, with the small 1960s vase and lamp stand in Barcelona Orange. The color combination is "hot" and shows how a little bit of orange goes a long, long way in this room. The colors do not clash, as they are in the same part of the color spectrum, but they make an arresting mix.

Janice's bohemian style is all about lots of seemingly wild colors that are actually well considered, and the careful choice of contrasting different elements in each room.

[opposite] The color composition is fabulous, mixing as it does the bright blue Indian enamel pitcher with the white and yellow bird motif, next to the 1960s graphite/orange vase on the Antibes Green side table. Note the table is finished with an Indian ceramic hand-painted drawer knob.

[above, left] Among clashing cultural references are the tribal horse hangings from India, displayed with rosary beads.

[above, right] The Victorian brass bed is covered with a brightly patterned Indian shawl, next to a classic 1960s orange table lamp with a green-yellow floral (flower power) patterned lampshade.

paint your own

Express yourself

Bohemian confidently takes references from different cultures and integrates them into a new mix. Taking references from other continents is what artists have been doing for centuries, so certainly having an artist in you and the confidence to make bold decisions makes boho work better. If you can pick up something and say, "I don't know why I like it but I love it," or "It's just what I want for my mantelpiece," and you have the confidence to say, "Why not put it there?" rather than, "Why would you put it there?" you are well on the way to being bohemian.

Ultimately, the bohemian home is a way of expressing your ideas—a bit of shouting out about a color or decorative piece. You might, for example, paint a wall in a striking color and cover it with contrasting pictures. Remember that after clashing cultures comes clashing colors. A riot of color is not essential—it can be restrained and still eye-catching (as with Janice's rooms). Contrasting and clashing patterns can work together, and liberties can be taken, as with the room scene shown opposite. What holds them together is the dominant Provence wall, supported by other shades of blue in the sofa fabric and throw.

The swatch I've suggested to mirror the color mix of the tabletop setting here contains Antibes Green, Provence, Burgundy with Old White, and Antibes Green again.

[opposite] Janice made the lampshade from a Russian scarf and she also painted the lamp stand. It is a perfect accompaniment to the Russian nesting doll, and all the elements are pulled together perfectly by the wall painted in Florence (which Janice says she could sit and look at all day).

Chapter 5
vintage floral

We find this by far the prettiest of all the room recipes. It is a wonderfully nostalgic style that evokes a time gone by, of simple elegance dominated by floral imagery. The vintage part goes back to the 1800s but its heyday is the Victorian and Edwardian era. More recent influences include the Arts and Crafts Movement, romantic Art Nouveau, abstract prints, as well as the vibrantly colored flowers of the 1960s and 1970s.

Floribunda, an abundance of flowers, is the defining element, with floral designs—predominantly roses—displayed on fabrics, bedcovers, upholstered chairs, cushion covers, wallpapers, and delicately designed china. The rose holds center stage—this and other floral motifs are inspired by the tradition of the English cottage garden, which we love. Real flowers, especially displayed in floral pitchers, as well as framed floral prints, are very much part of the mix. Other key ingredients include salvaged furniture, especially the worn look of French country pieces repainted in a distressed fashion, vintage toys and dolls, cut glass, and vintage bed linen.

Vintage floral is about telling a story, bringing history to life, and florals help to tell that story—you only have to think of the poppy and all that it evokes.

[opposite] This bedroom has all the classic elements of vintage floral— Victorian bed linen with roses, real roses in a cut-glass vase on a lace-covered side table, and several gilt-framed floral prints. White is the predominant background color, though the aquamarine window top works well for retro and country interiors. Use my Provence with Old White to make an equivalent color.

[above] A floribunda rose print and a purple side table frame these vintage floral pieces. The vintage packets are petal dust and were found unopened at a fair.

elements of vintage floral style

Colors

Vintage floral is all about the faded look—there are plenty of colors used, but they are not bright. Faded suggests vintage, the wear and tear that comes with reclaimed and nostalgic pieces. There is also an emphasis on light, pastel colors. Of course, color choice is highly personal, but there are some useful guidelines to follow if you are going for a classic rose-dominated vintage floral style. The colors should be as soft as the furnishings. Because floral patterns are the dominant motifs in the wallpaper design and paintings, the main wall and ceiling color needs to be a knocked-back white, or off-white, to soften the contrast and keep the room looking fresh and light.

The simplicity of white adds a delicate and romantic effect to room interiors, and vintage floral definitely has a touch of romance about it. Warm, off-whites look great against natural or bleached floorboards and exposed beams and window frames. They also add a soft glow to textured patterns, real flower arrangements, and embroidered cushion covers, bedcovers, and tablecloths. Decorating whites vary greatly in texture and tone, which gives you plenty to play with in paintwork, fabrics, floor coverings, and chinaware. It is certainly not a straitjacket, even if its primary function is to be a foil for the floral elements.

The quality of light is really important with vintage floral. It is a style that is mainly popular in temperate climates, so there is a natural inclination to use muted, softer colors anyway because it never gets that bright or hot. However, if you live in a hotter zone, it is natural to use vibrant colors in good, strong, bright light. Try to avoid these for the vintage floral look, as it can end up looking garish. Delicacy is the name of the game.

If you are going to introduce into the setting real flowers, such as roses, which, for the most part, come in glorious, rich hues, the impact of such colors needs to be set against neutral tones. Brilliant colors should be avoided because they will overpower or clash with the floral furnishings on display. Soft reds work well, especially next to neutrals, and like pinks and peaches they are warm and comforting colors that are pleasant and easy on the eye.

One last word on fabrics: While floral designs will feature strongly, you can also introduce plain and patterned and laced-edged white fabrics, such as bed linen and bedcovers. Vintage Victorian and Edwardian finds would make ideal furnishings.

In my artwork of vases, I've used purplish- and turquoisey-pinks and oranges and yellows—lovely, more fragile colors that are often forgotten. The swatch below shows how to use blues and greens, alongside different pinks.

[opposite] A variation on the vintage floral color palette is provided by this large modern room with its predominantly white floorboards and clapboard walls. The floral colors are provided by the pastel peach and pink hard chairs, the two-tone brown chair, and the deep pink cushion. The pale green table draws out the stronger green and purple flower arrangement.

[above and top] We like the color approach of these two rooms—the light, greeny-blues and soft whites on natural woods. Provence and Greek Blue are modern blues that also suit a retro style, and these pastel colors work particularly well in a bedroom. The arrangement of real flowers provides an additional vibrancy.

Patterns

Floribunda translates as "a plant, especially a rose, which bears dense clusters of flowers," and that is the signature motif and springboard for vintage floral patterns. It is inspired by the tradition of the English cottage garden but can take in classical continental French and Italian garden designs, as well as historic American gardens, and even tropical plants. While vintage floral patterns tend to revolve mainly around roses, there are plenty of other plants to showcase, especially those planted in herbaceous borders, including hollyhocks, delphiniums, and lupines.

Whichever flowers you fancy, they can be depicted in lots of different ways. They may be a classic still life or the rich, rather dense Victorian approach; they could be the later and lighter Charles Voysey-style textile designs, or the more modern floral twists by Pat Albeck, or they might even be a floral color scheme based on pastels.

The key to the patterns is that they should be subdued, calm, pretty, and not too alarming. In fact, one definition of vintage floral might be "nothing to scare the horses." The pattern of flowers might be set in lace or integrated as posies, bouquets, borders, or bunches. There is no

shortage of floral patterned wallpapers and coverings to source from design shops and junk shops. Wallpapering with vintage floral patterns is a quick way to get a pretty, romantic look in any room.

You might also try stencils; there are an amazing variety of floral patterns that you could incorporate into a vintage floral decorative wall pattern. It could be Arts and Crafts, Art Nouveau, or fun and funky 1960s style.

Built-in patterns are provided by vintage patchwork quilts and comforters (eiderdowns) with faded floral motifs, which you can source from boutiques and antique stores. They also make excellent wall hangings. The fabric may be chintz but it has to be faded chintz—new chintz won't cut it. However, if you have new chintz, then you could fade it or age it a bit by soaking it in tea, then washing it. Or you could dye it using an Annie Sloan Chalk Paint® (see pages 218–219). I have done this to great effect with French linen. Another option to create a faded pattern is to wash your chintz in Old White, dry it out, and then transfer an image that you can source from a decoupage motif book, an old

This chair has been upholstered with an eye-catching rose-patterned fabric called Dolores. The woodwork is painted with a lightened Chateau Grey. You could also simply cover a chair with a floral printed throw.

flower or plant book, or from the internet. Use my decoupage glue and varnish if you are going to try decoupage as a technique.

Floral patterns can be highlighted not just on textiles and wallpaper designs in delightful faded colors, but also on pillows, aprons, curtains, and lampshades. The canvas is as broad as you want it to be. Try to source floral patterns to create a romantic mood that evokes memories of ancient roses, charming old cottages, and endless summers.

[opposite] These rose-pink floral patterned cushions provide a romantic feel for this dreamy off-white paneled bedroom.

[right] A wall-mounted quilt shows more modern abstract floral patterns behind the bed, which has a traditional retro comforter (eiderdown).

I copied this floral pattern from a vintage border. Flower patterns can be reduced to a number of simple shapes, then filled with color.

Real flowers

From a single-stem, rich-red rose or tulip, to big, colorful blooms of freshly cut peonies, to displays of dried hydrangeas, the presentation of real flowers is a surefire way to complete any vintage floral room. The two key influences are the English cottage garden, with its neatly tended wild flowers and climbing roses on a whitewashed thatched cottage wall, and the rose itself, of which there are over 100 species. The rose is a nostalgic, romantic, homey, pre-industrialized symbol that still evokes a gentler age, hence its iconic status with vintage floral.

Cottage garden flowers include phlox, larkspur, and cornflowers, and popular flowers to consider for color variations or beautiful large blooms include chrysanthemums, lilies, tulips, dianthus (including carnations, pinks, and sweet Williams), gladioli, and peonies. Don't forget to add greenery, such as gypsophila or the silvery-blue foliage of *Eucalyptus gunnii*—both make fantastic fillers. Dried flowers work very well and, of course, have a much longer display life. Dried hydrangeas can look amazing with touches of russet, mauve, and crimson. Garlands of dried, real, or even synthetic flowers can also make a great visual impact hung on walls, doors, and windows.

To display flowers, choose vases that have a flower or vintage floral motif or flower shape. Cut glass is in keeping, and you can even opt for Japanese pottery designs.

[opposite] A beautiful Victorian pitcher with stylized floral designs displays a fabulous bouquet of fresh flowers, framed by an unadorned metal garden chair. It makes a lovely floral statement against this Antoinette wall.

[above] From left to right: A bunch of pink and orange roses are displayed in a Japanese vase to great effect; a single chrysanthemum sits in a vintage floral mug (these flowers are second only to roses in popularity); ranunculus and gypsophila are displayed in a white bowl that is petal-shaped—simple but highly effective.

back to her **roots**

This fascinating house is steeped in history. It was once owned by the artist Graham Sutherland, an official World War II artist, as well as an imaginative painter of landscapes and portraits. The current owner, Madeline Tomlinson, lived in the village as a child. She remembers the house well and seeing the artist painting in his attic studio.

The house is now adorned with Madeline's collectibles. They make up a wonderfully evocative vintage floral style that we found utterly enthralling and pleasing to the eye. The influence possibly comes from her very early life in London, living upstairs from her grandfather's florist's shop. She remembers the damp, fragrant smell of the flowers coming from the store below. Her great-grandmother was a flower seller in Covent Garden, so it's no wonder that Madeline is drawn to flowers.

Her style is floral and vintage, combined with a nostalgia for childhood and the romance of the past. Edwardian and Victorian pieces evoke a golden age of innocence. It is a fantasy world, a world evoked by the movies of Merchant Ivory, such as *A Room with a View*.

Madeline prefers strong colors that have faded over time. There are flowers everywhere, from fabric flowers on hats, to wallpaper patterns, to paintings. The result is a wonderfully cozy, delicate, pretty, old-fashioned floral style.

Vintage floral can easily translate into personal nostalgia. If you collect vintage items, whether toys or soft furnishings, this style forms the perfect backdrop to display your prized finds. It's all about the arrangement— as with these antique dolls, stuffed toys, and vintage linen.

The house is set in an idyllic, unspoilt village in Kent, a county that is traditionally known as the "Garden of England." It is a wonderful, white clapboard house; a big cottage with half timbers.

We entered from the back via a lovely, very well-kept garden. Because of her past, flowers are very evocative for Madeline. The vintage floral style she has adopted, however, is as much about her collection of nostalgic toys, teddy bears, dolls, and other items of a bygone era, as about being a homage to her florist family.

Madeline is not stuck-at-home wallowing in nostalgia; in fact, she travels frequently to France and the U.S., seeking out finds in antiques shows and flea markets. Whereas the sophisticated, well-traveled boho stylist would go abroad and bring back items and influences to sit next to— and purposefully clash with—other pieces, Madeline always returns to her roots in terms of her finds. She is adding to, and complementing, an already established theme. So the house is chock-a-block with vintage and nostalgic finds, all lovingly displayed, that add to another layer

A SHOWCASE FOR
NOSTALGIA

[previous page] The large quilt hanging behind the classic Victorian brass bed is impressive with its flower petal-inspired shapes. The quilted bedcover and pillows have charming, light pink rose designs.

[opposite] This spare bedroom is a potpourri of vintage items. There are floral motifs from the real flowers and the framed watercolors of flower arrangements. Many of the antique pieces on the shelves were bought from trade fairs, flea markets, and junk shops, specifically to display. The train and teddy bear were her husband's as a boy, so there is plenty of personal nostalgia here too.

[above, left] On the other side of the spare bedroom, the exposed 16th-century wall joists are classic English cottage style, while the overhead beams have been painted to blend in with the ceiling. A bunkbed becomes a shelving display for an assortment of antique linen and covers, as well as a toy dog and a wooden toy caravan.

[above, right] The arrangement of the floral Edwardian bag with the umbrella is the epitome of vintage floral.

of the recipe. Madeline has carefully chosen all the furniture and furnishings, well worn or attractively floral in design, to suggest stories and highlight a heritage.

This old English cottage is fortunate to still have many original timber wall and ceiling beams, in their natural faded browns or painted in soft whites and greens. The dominant colors are poppy red, delphinium blue, and rose pink. The walls are pale whites or off-white, and most spaces are filled with Victorian and Edwardian floral watercolors, oils, and prints. There is plenty of antique white linen to provide a laundry-white freshness.

Since moving in some 14 years ago, Madeline has decorated the interior beautifully. She has also acquired an amazing collection of original, antique, floral-patterned quilts, comforters, wooden and metal toys, porcelain dolls, and stuffed teddy bears.

For people like Madeline, the vintage floral style is about having fun, by buying or upcycling vintage items and styles that you love from an era faded in history, and by making a home a comfy, relaxing, even romantic retreat, which, above all, is unique to you.

IT'S ALL IN THE DETAIL

We went across from the spare room upstairs into Madeline's charming old farmhouse bedroom. The magnificent quilted cover on the bed provides the focus but it is the way Madeline has arranged the soft furnishings around the room, while highlighting the exposed rustic wall joists and ceiling beams, that gives this room its charm and delicacy. Her attention to detail is amazing. She has thought it through from purchase to display and yet managed to keep it all understated.

Madeline's style in this room is very much about collecting—but not exclusively—floral-inspired furnishings that please the eye in their arrangement, as well as their complementary colors.

Everything in this room has been personally sourced as an antique: the kimono dressing gown, the oil painting of flowers, the floral lampshade, the Liberty print dress, the pillowcases, and the Cheramy print, which is an old eau de cologne advertisement. The blue chintz curtains work well here, even though they may not be in the traditional faded flower palette. Other blue-tinted pieces add to a sense of calm. In true vintage floral style, there are flowers everywhere, including a bouquet displayed on the windowsill.

If you want to emulate this style for a bedroom, you could start with a linen-and-lace look of the past to add a vintage mood. A decoratively trimmed pillowcase or comforter in a soft rose or cream shade is also a great way to get the look.

[opposite] Everything is old and antique in this room; there is nothing new. Even the anglepoise lamp is a vintage find, rather than a store-bought reproduction. Authenticity is important to Madeline, but for those on smaller budgets, floral ephemera can be sourced quite cheaply and used imaginatively.

[above, right] This doll in an old suitcase was bought at an antique fair in the U.S. The display ensemble is what really works here, revealing all the old fabric inside the suitcase, which is just exquisite, and complemented by the antique floral print on which it rests.

[right] A random baby's shoe, dried purple berries, and antiquarian books hark back to a bygone era. Madeline's color palette includes a lot of quite bright reds and pinks.

The bathroom's centerpiece (literally) is the freestanding Victorian tub with shower and net curtain. It evokes a time gone by when life (and possibly plumbing!) was simpler. The floral motifs are restrained but the style is definitely vintage. As soon as we saw it, we thought this central-stage bathtub was amazing.

Again Madeline has shown a real attention to detail, in the faucets (taps), the freestanding soap bracket, and all the other touches. The exposed old timber joists and off-white color scheme provide a very intimate and relaxing space.

The adjacent toilet has some cleverly positioned floral-patterned additions against an all-white surround that continues the old-fashioned feel (not least with the Victorian-look lavatory itself).

[opposite] This is part of the attic studio where artist Graham Sutherland, the former owner, might have sat and looked out at the garden. The little alcove has a padded window seat in red gingham and several large, blue, floral-designed cushions.

[above, left] The superb, free-standing Victorian bathtub with lion-paw feet is a striking feature of the room.

[above, right] A lady's flowery dressing gown hangs from a door hook, while an antique standard lamp base becomes a hat stand. Both items help to soften the old-fashioned-looking toilet. The floral print on the back wall and the glass bottles complete the cottage-like feel.

HOME COMFORTS

Downstairs is dominated by a very large, L-shaped sitting room, with exposed timber beams. Where a partition wall has been knocked through to make the room larger is a fabulous painted wall panel that may have been created by Graham Sutherland's wife. It is a superb feature for the vintage floral setting with its swirling plant motifs.

The overall creamy white look is very soothing and allows plenty of scope for the floral soft furnishings dotted around the room. The backing to the central comfy chair has a rich purplish-red that really stands out against the other muted colors, as do the striking flower arrangements. The cushions are classic floral designs, with the red rose as the central image. There are plenty of floral and white patterned cushions dotted around the cream sofa. Together with the cream carpet and painted wooden coffee table and display cabinet, this says "comfy cottage" in the extreme. The standard lamp is pure nostalgia, and the shade has a delightful floral pattern. To the right behind the lampshade you can see

[above] The flowers and flower-inspired furnishings have been carefully laid out to create a cosy, comfy, and gentle-on-the-eye interior space.

[right] Doing a floral pattern on a white background is much harder than doing it on color. This background gives you something to bounce color ideas off and gives body to your work.

[opposite] The painted wall panel, possibly created by Graham Sutherland's wife, is a unique and inspiring piece. The vertical line is continued by the vintage lamp stand, with floral motifs on the shade.

The exquisitely designed floral quilt and the charmingly decorated antique toy horses have been curated to evoke a past that is treasured.

a vintage hardware-store display of storage trays that would originally have held nails, screws, and other iron goods. Again, this is the idea of showcasing history and heritage and bringing it alive. At the other end of the sitting room is a space absolutely packed with vintage and floral items. Madeline has placed a doll's house in pink and green next to neatly folded floral blankets and quilts—all authentic antiques—on top of a highly distressed wooden cupboard. She has taken her childhood inspirations and proudly displayed their heritage. This is very much a vintage statement. Furniture that shows its age, such as a highly crackled painted cupboard, is an integral part of this look, and the patina is very much part of the charm of the room.

The shelving inside the cupboard is packed with even more vintage floral covers and counterpanes! Beside this is a wonderful early 20th-century metal toy car, in which the child would pedal and steer (outdoors). Next to that is a toy horse on wheels below a beautiful rich red floral table cover. There is a touch of a set design for the TV series *Downton Abbey*—and that is nothing if not pure vintage and nostalgia.

[opposite] A dummy's head stares somewhat forlornly from the bottom of this extremely aged and very crackled cupboard, rammed with vintage blankets and covers. The rest of the dummy's body stands rather poignantly beside it. A small toy horse on wheels rests below the rich red floral table cover. The doll's house is painted in a charming combination of light green and light pink—very complementary colors. It's a combination I like. It works in several other styles and it's one I've used happily on several pieces.

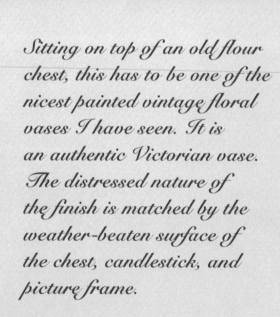

Sitting on top of an old flour chest, this has to be one of the nicest painted vintage floral vases I have seen. It is an authentic Victorian vase. The distressed nature of the finish is matched by the weather-beaten surface of the chest, candlestick, and picture frame.

WORKING VINTAGE

We walked through to the light, airy kitchen with its Victorian range set on flagstone tiles. This ubiquitous style of country kitchen provides the cottagey backbone to this room with its cast-iron, enamel-glazed design that hasn't changed since the 1920s. This is about as working vintage as you can get.

The large, white tablecloth with red floral trimming is the perfect platform to show off the tea cozy and hydrangea display in the light blue bucket. Both are classic vintage floral. The upholstered dining chairs are very complementary, having muted floral designs. The focal point is a rather quirky "3 Blues" advertising sign which, though not strictly floral, is certainly vintage. We thought it might be a fairground shooting gallery sign indicating that if you hit three blues, you'd win a prize.

[opposite, top left] The highly distressed, vintage blue shutters and lamp base can be re-created but these are original. The shutters come from the South of France, where a variety of bright and muted blues and greens are common. Florence and Provence can be mixed to make a similar color. The palette is a mix of cool blues and a cool white with tiny drops of warm pinks and reds.

[opposite, center, and below] A turn-of-the-century selection of antique finds, including a floral plate, potpourri jar, and book collection. A later modern variation comes with this set of floral-inspired objects and fabrics.

[above] The kitchen is country-inspired with a simple color scheme of white and red predominating. The large beam in front of the range has been painted white, which keeps the room light. Around the table are some painted French chairs.

Copying patterns

There is an air of an elegant past that often defines vintage floral, and this setting has it in heaps. Furniture that shows its age, such as a well-worn painted side table, is an integral part of this look, as is a hardware store's set of drawers above it. Some items displayed are expensive, but if you have a good eye, you can find some great rare pieces at flea markets, antique stores, and auctions that will add interest and give your home a vintage floral identity.

Here we have a beautifully decorated chest of drawers, with an Eastern European folky feel about it but still centered around floral motifs. This would not be difficult to copy on a plain piece of furniture because, if you look closely at the detail (inset), you'll see it is made up of a number of quite simple patterns, and so you can quite easily re-create those patterns yourself, building them up as you go along.

My artwork shows the basic flowers, swirls, and even simple dots that are all seen on this chest of drawers. Build the flowers up step by step, letting them dry in between each stage. For the swirls, making notches at regular intervals, as I have done (along the top of the brown artwork), will enable you to keep them all the same size.

[above] The numbers on the blue background are a sequence of steps to show how to copy the painted flowers on the chest of drawers. The background color is Aubusson and the flowers are English Yellow and Old White. The border is Primer Red and Barcelona Orange with a yellow pattern.

[opposite] Whichever vintage floral items you decide to go for, creating the look is more about the way you display them and how those items invite someone to consider the story behind them. On top of the drawers is a Victorian bell jar housing delicate wax plants. Possibly a one-off find, it tells a fascinating tale. Hanging on the wall is the front panel of a doll's house which is a very beautiful object in its own right.

[left] Using the correct brushes is important. You need a soft, fine-haired brush that comes to a point. Step 1 shows how you first make a wide, fat shape—push hard to do this. In step 2, pull the brush back, using less pressure, to end with a point. Always add water to the paint—just enough to make it flow.

Chapter 6

french elegance

When it comes to elegance, the French have a knack for just oozing it, whether in fashion or furnishings. For us, there are two sides to French elegance. There is the gilded elegance and understated grandeur of the French, and then the earthy, rustic, rural French home. The words "simple" and "uncluttered" define this style, and we witnessed firsthand a superb example of it in the center-west of France (see the room on the opposite page). A light, delicate touch in everything is very much part of this sophisticted style too.

The chateau look often displays furniture and furnishings that are rococo in style—rococo refers to the natural curves found in shells. The turned look and the gorgeously curved cabriole leg are also part of the slightly frivolous and light-touch nature of the style.

French elegance is a design style that has been hugely influential on interior decorating for hundreds of years, and in recent times it has become even more popular because it seems to work so well. Personally, we find the light colors, the French decor, and the sense of minimalism very alluring—so much so, I now have a house in rural France, which tries to be elegant too!

[opposite] A rounded and upholstered bed is the centerpiece for this very beautifully understated room. There is a sort of minimalism about French decor, and this bedroom displays it well, together with the signature light colors. The linen curtains are very simple, and the room is neat and uncluttered.

[above] This kitchen has elements of rustic style, but the sign above the sink and the simple fabric below are singularly French.

elements of french elegance style

Texture

The unadorned and crisp nature of the surfaces are accentuated by texture. Because the colors used in French elegance tend to be on the pale side, the texture comes out and shows through in room interiors and on decorative pieces. The finish is matte, with only a few hints of sheen. This style, like French cuisine, relies on fresh ingredients. Natural materials abound, with not just wood, but metal, stone, and terracotta, combined with matte paints and washes, rather than any arty or artificial, shiny finishes.

Fabrics, too, can be very tactile, especially old French striped mattress ticking material and linens, so having plenty of cushions and pillowcases in such materials certainly adds to the overall textured feel of a room. French ticking originated as a hands-on fabric to cover mattresses,

pillows, and daybeds. It is an extremely durable fabric. It was originally woven to withstand the ends of feathers piercing through and for general heavy use. It traditionally has a sturdy weave and straight-line pattern.

As with many houses in France, especially country houses, the walls are built of stone. A textured wall can look beautiful, and the cracks highlighted and made into a feature if they are painted over with diluted Old White, Paris Grey, or another light color. You can re-create the weathered, washed, and naturally faded-paint look using my paints and some very simple techniques.

If you decide to paint a rough stone wall, you'll find the first coat will be easily absorbed and dry quickly, so just go back and apply an extra

[left] Highly textured French shutters become a feature for the inside of this light, creamy-white living room in the south of France. The neutral palette of creams, whites, beiges, and grays is calm and soothing and a perfect backdrop for the rough stone walls, exposed whitewashed beams, wooden ceiling, and limestone slabs. The hand-woven linens are very French style. The whole look is natural, simple, and not at all precious.

coat of paint till you get the desired effect. For 1 liter of paint, mix in 1 liter of water in a bucket and stir with a clean stick. Brush the surface with water first, as this will help to absorb the paint and draw it into the wall. Brush the paint in, dabbing with the bristles to get to all the crevices and cracks. Be prepared for quite a bit of paint dribbling.

If you want to retain the patina of textured wood but give it a whitewashed French feel, paint the surface with a brush, working in the direction of the wood. Before the area has had time to dry, wipe it with a circular motion using a clean, dry cloth, until you have the textured effect you are looking for. How much paint you need and how much rubbing will depend on the type of wood and whether it is new or old.

[above, left] Some of my very old French pewter spoons, on which the decoration and flourishes are on the underside. Apparently, this is because a French king once caught the prongs of the fork on his lace cuff sleeves when eating, so he declared the prongs must be face down. So all silverware faces down, with the decoration on the other side facing up!

[above, right] This worn-away and whitewashed wooden table in my French house is positioned against a very textured wall, which I have rolled and sponged using a damask-style stencil.

This collection of old French plates shows an amazing variety of whites, which is partly due to the different textures. Some of the plates are quite matte, almost like stone, and others have a shiny finish. French plates are great to source for decoration—I collect them all the time.

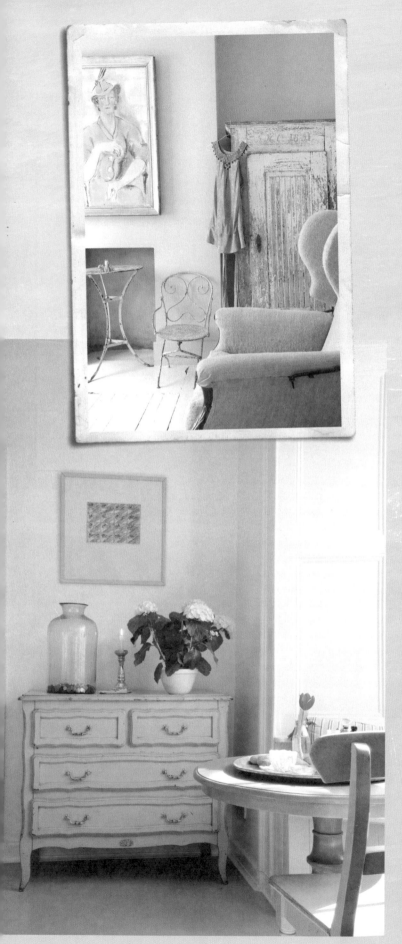

Rococo curves

Rococo is a style based on shells and the way they curve. This pretty style developed in the 18th century, when it pricked the pomposity of the classical style with its playfulness. It lightened the form with symmetrical curves and became quite free-form, using rocks (*rocailles*) and shells (*coquilles*) as the decorative motifs, based on those found in the fountains and grottoes of the gardens of Versailles. Rococo borrows from nature, so you will see leaves and flowers intertwined with rocks and shells in elaborate outlines. Mirrors, small tables, consoles, and chandeliers lend themselves well to this style. Gilt bronze, gilded carving, lines of color, or inlay could also be used to draw lines together in curved sequences.

Cabriole legs very much distinguish the style. Cabriole is usually singled out for furniture—shaped legs in a double curve with the upper part swelling out, while the curve swings in toward the foot, which again flares out. Its use in French (and European) furniture started in the late 17th century, with effort being put into varying the familiar turned and square legs. Some styles used scrolls and animal feet, but the better-known designs made the whole leg into an abstract, sinuous line. It can be very pleasing to the eye and helps define a French elegance interior.

Chandeliers are a great showcase for the frivolous nature of this style. It's complete fantasy—the upper-class romantic idea of the countryside. You can pick up simple versions, even ones to hold candles, in *brocantes* and junk shops, and give them a paint makeover or accentuate their textured and rococo appeal. The toile de Jouy pattern is similarly romantic. Toile is named after the 18th-century factory of Jouy-en-Josas, but you'll recognize it by those traditional patterns you see on fabrics depicting pastoral scenes of farmers working in the fields, couples picking apples in an orchard, and even the Montgolfier Brothers in their hot-air balloon. We love this centuries-old textile tradition so much that we have used it as the template for our new fragrance collection designs.

[above, left] The iron table and chair both have rococo curves, as does the oversized 19th-century French wingback armchair.

[left] A pretty French chest of drawers, which is of no great age or worth, has been newly painted with curved edges and wiggles, so there are no straight edges anywhere. This look is so rococo—why have a straight line when you can have something more decorative?

[opposite] This room has a warm palette—the walls have been faux-finished with a soft gray hue. This texture and color are complementary to the more earthy-colored furniture and furnishings, including the chairs, the mirrors, and the chandelier. At the fore of the photo, around the table, you can see some fine French toile de Jouy.

[right] I've illustrated some swatches based on bergère armchairs. Bergère means "shepherdess" in French, and it's thought the name may have come from French aristocrats loving to act the rustic shepherd and shepherdess! I've used fairly strong pale colors—from left to right: Emile, Antoinette with Henrietta, Old Ochre, Versailles, and Louis Blue.

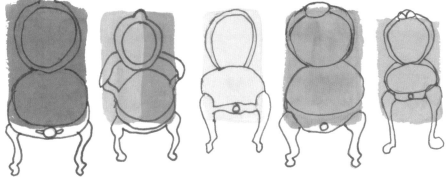

Colors

I have been hugely influenced by the natural palette of France and French styles, which tends to take in a range of extremely attractive, semi-pale colors. Many of my Annie Sloan Chalk Paints® are directly inspired by the French style as the litany of French names and place names attests: Napoleonic Blue, Provence, Burgundy, Arles, and Antibes Green, to name a few. And then there are my wonderful neutrals—Chateau Grey and French Linen. Decorative French styles in the 18th century have particularly inspired my selection of several paint colors, including Aubusson Blue, Antoinette, Henrietta, and Duck Egg Blue.

So I have a natural affinity with French elegance, and my paints will be a perfect highlight and foil for room interiors and painted furniture in this style. I have also suggested a palette based on typical south of France colors (see opposite).

Colors are not just influenced by painted furniture and walls but also by the strong tradition of French textiles, especially the old mattress ticking, with its gorgeous, mainly blue and white stripes, and the beautiful old embroidered dishtowels, pillowcases, and sheets.

The tradition of embroidery is very strong in France. It was something every young French girl was taught in school, as this antique embroidered alphabet shows.

[opposite] The harmonious colors of this interior are led by the textural elements of the wooden wall and floorboards. The distressed wooden bench has been transformed into a comfortable sofa with the addition of a squab and cushions made out of a collection of old grain sacks.

[above, left] Like the other two pictures above, this is of my Normandy house. It shows the kitchen through to the sitting room, painted in Provençal colors, including Old White, Chateau Grey, and, naturally enough, Provence for the door.

[above, center] The lily of the valley, commonly known as *muguet* in French, is celebrated every May 1 as *La Fête du Muguet*, and is part of the Labor Day public holiday. A tradition of giving lily of the valley flowers is supposed to have begun on May 1, 1561, when King Charles IX was presented with a bunch of them as a token of luck and prosperity for the coming year. He, in turn, began the custom of presenting lily of the valley flowers to the ladies of his court each year on May 1.

[above, right] Two typical Breton cider cups hang on this distressed panel that I painted.

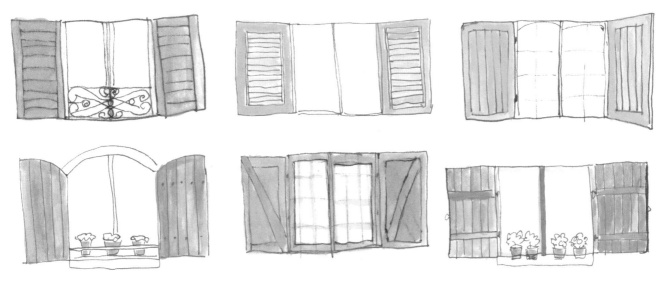

My swatch of colors for French elegance based on south of France shutter designs. From top, left to right: Provence, Arles, Antibes Green; bottom, left to right: Coco with white, Florence, a mix of Louis Blue and Napoleonic Blue.

the romantic school

To say we were stunned when we first laid eyes on the interiors of Alex Russell Flint's home is something of an understatement. This young artist-painter lives and works in this rambling former schoolhouse in Argenton-Château. It is located about 186 miles (300km) south of Paris—not on the tourist trail—in the Deux-Sèvres (Poitou-Charentes region) in the center-west of France. The village is beautiful, set in a valley, with a river, the Argenton, running through it. This big, old building is perched on a hillside and commands great views.

The building dates mainly from 1850, but there are older and newer bits. It is a treat to behold, and suits Alex to a tee. He told us that, as a child, he loved to make dens, and nothing has changed as far as he is concerned. He still loves messing about, being creative with rooms and images, and getting a buzz out of it. That is certainly evident in both his paintings and room interiors. There is a romantic and rustic tinge to his French elegance. The room shown opposite, believe it or not, is his kitchen. It is quite a quirky setup, with the daybed holding up a traditional ceiling clothes dryer—and it is a really high ceiling.

Alex bought the property from a friend in 2010. He still has loads of work to do on it. One claim to fame for the house is that it was lived in for a time by Bernadette Lafont, the first female star of the French cinema's *Nouvelle Vague* (New Wave) movement.

You can enter the house at ground level or from the floor above because it sits on a steep hillside. We came in via the upper-floor back entrance and were immediately captivated by the sense of space, the simple but well-chosen elements of decoration, and the quiet and subdued color tones. Even the vintage tricolor flags are not heavy-handed.

The pockmarked walls provide a perfect backdrop for Alex's display of carefully chosen paintings, mirrors, and found objects. He loves to collect bits and pieces from *vide-greniers* (flea markets), *brocantes,* and *salons d'antiquaires* (antique stores). There are French flags, kids' toys, an old birdcage—these objects may not be elegant in themselves, but Alex has put them together and presented them in a very elegant way.

Many of the paintings are his own and some are by his grandfather, Sir William Russell Flint, especially known for his watercolor paintings of women. The walls also feature several old school posters that are an apt reminder that the building was once a schoolhouse.

FRENCH FITTINGS

[previous page] Part of the beautiful kitchen with its wonderful high ceiling. It is laid out simply with a very pale Provence paneled background.

[above] One of the back entrances into the house, showing the lovely proportions of the old schoolhouse. The highly textured walls are not at all perfectly filled and have a rustic elegance, especially in their understated yellow ocher color.

[opposite] This arrangement of objects is a more rustic take on French elegance, but elegant nonetheless. There are beautiful gold picture frames, an old birdcage, a child's toy, and books, all set against a beautifully textured wall.

The found objects Alex has collected are eclectic but all have a French feel, not least the Catholic crucifix on the wall above the door mantel through to his studio. The child's tricycle appears to be arranged randomly but, like many of the items in the studio, it is there to become a reference for a still life or to practice a quick sketch.

The door itself shows the two sides of French elegance. The finely paneled door facing outside the studio is a uniform and simple cream color, offset by the strong, clean, green lines of the panel frames. That lends a simple elegance to the corridor. The other side of the door, which is inside the studio, is quite different in color and texture. It blends much more with the studio's interior, with its distressed and weathered Aubusson Blue washed color.

The daybed, with its bright red mattress, looks like a French vintage hospital bed, with the very typical French mattress ticking pillows. This textured material was stitched and woven in multiple directions to stop feathers poking through, and the interwoven mesh has a nice, crisp feel to it.

FRENCH FINDS

[previous page] A view of Alex's studio, which is the heart of the house. The interior is simply stunning and not just because it shows an amazing mix of Annie Sloan paints, which Alex has used very freely—slapping on Aubusson Blue, a little bit of Greek Blue, and Burgundy too. Alex has also scraped the woodwork on the door to create a sympathetically textured finish that goes with the whole room. The result is simple elegance.

[opposite] Aubusson Blue features on the baseboard (skirting board) wall molding in the studio, the studio door architrave, and the glass-framed corridor doors, giving a neat sense of continuity.

[above] A close-up of the wrought-iron daybed, most likely an old hospital bed. The wood burner is cast iron and has a simple, elegant design.

SIMPLE ELEGANCE

The kitchen is spacious and more on the rustic side of French elegance. This room is all about simplicity, with the cast-iron range providing the focus in front of the vast wall. The wall itself is painted in a neutral color, so that the items on it, including the mirror, old print, and glass-fronted wall cabinet, stand out. The metal pendant ceiling light has a classic, simple, and functional design and is very much in keeping with the raw materials and rustic durability of the French elegance style. On the left wall is one of several educational posters that Alex has sourced and hung up around the house.

Within the house, there is a self-contained apartment with its own kitchen and washing facilities. Although there are quite a number of accessories displayed in this setting, they have been very well spaced to avoid any sense of overcrowding or cluttering. The room has a very measured and relaxed look.

[above] The kitchen offers beautiful views from its ceiling-high windows. The full-length curtains are very simply designed and show their Louis Blue color to good effect. A nice touch is provided by the burlap (hessian) potato sacks acting as cupboard screens. The French educational poster in the corner is highly apt, given the house was once a school.

[opposite] A view of the separate apartment, which has a kitchenette, with a washstand, all in a simple French style. We especially liked the vintage Art Nouveau-style "Pfaff" soap-dish lettering.

[above, left] The linen-aproned washstand is a simply contoured bathroom accessory, especially with the Delft blue tiles. But it is the stripped-back, green-washed wall that is the dominant feature here. High up on the wall, the period, educational poster on teeth adds a tongue-in-cheek element.

[above, right] The wood-framed educational poster is a nice touch for a former school, and there are quite a few of these dotted around the house.

[opposite, above] At the back of the kitchen is this quite warehouse-style room, with the wooden crate put on casters and repurposed as a magazine rack, an old tin basin acting as a wood bucket, and the old leather chair with its stripy soft furnishings. Notice the vintage French antique "Allumettes" matches holder on the wall to the right.

We entered another bathroom in which Alex had taken off all the wallpaper to reveal a marvelous green color—similar to my Antibes Green—on the uneven surface. On one wall, Alex has actually used Antibes to match the part of the wall that shows the original distressed color. A light green is also employed on the sitting room's much smoother wall. On this, Alex has hung some beautiful framed paintings, as well as some whimsical items, including a set of oars.

Alex has chosen subtle and elegant tones for the painted ceilings, walls, and woodwork, and created a simple, seamless backdrop for his *brocante* buys. It's a very assured look that enhances and fits the large space exquisitely. And that's no mean feat, since he has taken on a really large building with a lot of rooms, which he has had to adjust and fine-tune on a tight budget.

The sitting room displays a timeless elegance. Although there are many paintings and other artifacts displayed on the wall, and a few furniture items, the large, plain, muted green wall and earthy wood floor help make the room seem remarkably uncluttered.

Upstairs, again with a superb view over the valley of Argenton, is possibly my favorite bathroom ever in the history of the world! This is so beautiful in its simplicity and clutter-free setting.

The double-ended roll-top tub is painted in Primer Red and cloaked by a magnificent mattress ticking in red and white, acting as a shower curtain. The heavy material is hung on an antique horse divider. This would have been used traditionally to keep plow horses in a straight line and at the same consistent distance apart. This is certainly an imaginative adaptation of traditional French mattress material and French farming implements—and it is done with French panache.

PERFECT PAINT

Alex Russell Flint describes himself as a contemporary realist painter in oils, and this is the first house he's ever owned. He's fallen in love with interior decoration, as you can tell, and has discovered Annie Sloan Chalk Paints®—he said it was the paint he'd been looking for but didn't know existed!

He said he loves the matte finish that our paint gives to a wall, especially as his walls are quite badly damaged. It's very forgiving and does not get highlights on every crack, so the very chalky finish is great and allows the artistic expression he is seeking that fits each room. The beautiful interior shot of the studio shows exactly how you can slap it straight on virtually anything, while allowing the walls to breathe, and create a great effect.

[opposite] The simple but elegant bathroom has an eye-catching vintage French mattress ticking converted into a make-do shower curtain. Traditionally, the tight-weave fabric is striped more often in blues; this red stripe is simply stunning.

[above, right] This attic space painted in Burgundy makes a delightful little bedroom.

[right] I absolutely love this tiny toilet under the stairs, with its old *Paris Match* magazine covers. I'd like to do this myself but that would be copying! If you have vintage magazines in a box and don't know what to do with them, this is a brilliant idea. The little wall cupboard is painted in Olive with Emperor's Silk on the inside; the wooden loo seat is also matched in Olive.

paint your own

Washed wall finish

Alex used my paints to create this beautifully washed wall, so it will be relatively easy for you to try your hand at a similar version. I've outlined here the colors that Alex used but try your own combination and don't be afraid to experiment with different color palettes.

To create this striking color and effect, Alex mixed Burgundy Red, Greek Blue, and Old White, possibly with a bit of Aubusson Blue (as in the inset picture). He then washed it and allowed some to drip down to extend it and give it texture. The chalky finish looks superb and absolutely fitted the bespoke look that Alex was seeking.

The paintings on the wall are Alex's own. The freestanding, 19th-century zinc bathtub may seem a humorous touch that adds a bit of eccentricity, but as an artist, Alex needs plenty of found items to inspire him—and not just the skull on the mantelpiece! He also bathes in the tub, so it is functional as well as stylish.

[right] This swatch of colors, as used by Alex to create the wonderful wall finish, is a mixture of Burgundy Red (Primer Red would do), Greek Blue, and Old White, possibly with a bit of Aubusson Blue. But the beauty of using my paints is that you can experiment with your own palette, so be bold!

Chapter 7

RUSTIC COUNTRY

We are very fond of the rustic country style. It's one that we've introduced into our own home in France. "Country" is all about celebrating the great outdoors away from the city, and if there's one style that brings the outside inside, it is this one. "Rustic" relates to our atavistic (we like this word) association and working relationship with the land. So this is a hands-on, down-to-earth, make-do style, where natural materials and deep, rich colors, especially earthy ochers, abound.

With rustic country, you won't find your romantic or pretty Jane Austen cottage in the country (that's probably more floral retro). The style may, however, include a few elements of Mr. Darcy's stately home, as some of the affluent end of the style can be quite smart and upscale.

It's the rustic side that gives this style its character. Think of the rough end of the country-house spectrum—the gamekeeper's cottage, the fisherman's cottage, the park keeper's and lockkeeper's lodges, as well as the hunting lodges, and, not least, the farmworker's humble home.

The furniture and furnishings in rustic country tend to be well worn and previously used—for example, in a bakery, forge, cowshed, or barn. It is also a style deeply embedded in North America—picture those rustic cabins in the woods and on the lakes.

[opposite] Our kitchen in France displays many rustic elements, including an old cider barrel I've hand-painted, handmade country pitchers, an old English church pew, a French log basket, a cushion cover made of old French mattress fabric, and a very battered Louis Vuitton trunk.

[above] A framed photograph of an old Breton fisherman is displayed on a workbench. Using a workbench indoors as a table is definitely a rustic statement. This one has a vintage metal vise for holding wood to drill holes into or to cut. A simple bunch of apple blossom and hedgerow flowers is also in keeping with the rustic country style.

ELEMENTS OF **RUSTIC COUNTRY** STYLE

FURNITURE AND ACCESSORIES

In rustic country, the furniture and accessories are sourced from the working countryside —from farmyards, barns, workshops, and other outbuildings—and brought straight into the home. By the same token, with this style many pieces of interior furniture and furnishings are placed outdoors. A lot of the fixtures and fittings come from farmhouses—we speak from personal experience, having scoured the *brocantes* of northern France, where I source traditional, rural community pieces and where, very often, the *brocantes* are actually sited in old barns.

Rustic country furniture, therefore, tends to be quite basic and simple in the way it is made. Tables, sideboards, and chairs will be chunky, sturdy, and built-to-last pieces. Table and chair legs will not be turned with lots of detail and carvings, for example. They would have been made fairly quickly, using local and homestead materials. They would serve an immediate need or function and be hard-working—made to take a beating! These sturdy pieces can take knocks, have bits missing, be scratched and

still look the part! There might also be some smarter items, such as gilt-framed mirrors, old upholstered chairs, and other pieces from the "grand house at the other end of the drive," but even these will not be overly done up. A concession to style might be a chair having a curved back, but it won't have lots of "curly" details or ornate flourishes. With rustic country, there is nothing fancy or adorned. A barrel becoming a table or a chair is much more in keeping.

Handmade wooden kitchen utensils are classic rustic accessories, displayed in all their worn glory in old cups and pitchers or hanging from ceiling racks. Old wooden plate and mug racks, vintage wooden clotheshorses for drying, and traditional wooden indoor drying racks on a pulley are good examples of rustic accessories. Enamel water pitchers and metal milk pitchers, wicker baskets, wire-shaped holders for collecting eggs, string bags for carrying fruit and vegetables in the kitchen garden, and river fishing implements are all natural inclusions for this style.

[above, left] A pewter pitcher sits on this workbench—you can see the drill holes and saw marks on this very used piece. To clean it up, I gave it a wash of Old White.

[above, center] We used this oil lamp for decoration in all its rusty, rustic beauty. I find it a very beautiful object, especially set in the deeply recessed, creamy-white window ledge with old paintwork.

[above, right] Some old battered French spoons lie on top of a cider barrel. Silverware and kitchen utensils are a common rustic country accessory.

I INSTANTLY LIKED THIS OLD COUNTRY POT, WHICH I FOUND IN FRANCE. IT SITS IN FRONT OF MY ROUGH-AND READY PAINTWORK. THE OLD WOOD HAD OIL-BASED PAINT, BUT I DIDN'T WANT TO STRIP IT BACK. INSTEAD, I DECIDED TO DECORATE IT WITH THIS PAINTED PICTURE.

THE COUNTRY INFLUENCE HERE IS DECIDEDLY SWEDISH, WITH THIS FARMHOUSE BLUE COLOR AND THE GUSTAVIAN ELEMENTS, NOT LEAST THE MORA CLOCK. THE SISAL RUG IS VERY "EARTHY" IN COLOR AND TEXTURE. A PIECE OF SACKCLOTH SLUNG OVER THE BACK OF A CHAIR BEARS ITS ORIGINAL STAMP.

COLORS

Traditionally, a simple palette of strong primary colors tends to dominate rustic country. These were the rough-and-ready pigments that were available to working countrymen and women. Light colors were avoided, except in the case of whitewashing—farmhouses and barns would be whitewashed once a year.

Whitewash is a caustic substance, used in the dairy shed and other working areas (traditionally, whitewashing meant using lime paint, which did not contain much pigment; it was thin and watery and so showed through the wood, as well as running off down the wall). Country folk would do the whitewashing in one go, including the furniture. It killed all the bugs, and any leftover would be used in the house, rather than having to paint individual items white. The whole point was to spend as little money as possible—to slap it on, to just cover the surface. Whitewashing is a messy task as it all dribbles onto the floor.

The modern equivalent of whitewashing is a "fresh up" wash (not with lime these days), and my Chalk Paint® approach is Old White

thinned or watered down. For it to seep in properly, it has to be used over wood that is unvarnished .

Furniture was painted in deep colors to protect it—examples might be dark, strong greens, deep blues, browny-reds, and oranges. The colors used were basically cheap ones, especially ochers (using the local earth as a pigment), hence the predominance of earthy colors with this style.

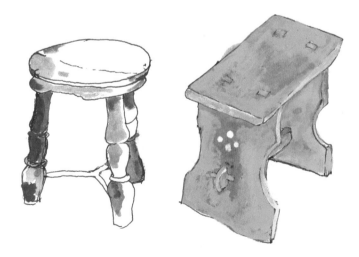

I'VE ILLUSTRATED FIVE ENAMEL PITCHERS (QUINTESSENTIAL RUSTIC PIECES) IN, FROM LEFT TO RIGHT: A YELLOWY, PALE OLD OCHRE, VERY MUCH AN EARTH COLOR; A GREENY-AUBUSSON BLUE, WHICH WAS A VERSATILE 19TH-CENTURY PAINT; PROVENCE, USED ESPECIALLY IN FRANCE, WHICH IS A PALE, LIGHTISH-BLUE (ADD A BLUEY-GREEN PIGMENT TO THE WHITEWASH); A BRIGHT RED, WHICH WAS POPULAR PARTICULARLY ON FARMHOUSE FURNITURE—EITHER PRIMARY RED EARTH PIGMENT OR A BRIGHT 19TH-CENTURY RED WITH OLD WHITE (THE LAST ENAMEL PITCHER). SUCH ENAMELWARE (IT COULD BE A COLANDER) IS RELATIVELY CHEAP AND CHANCES ARE YOU WILL FIND IT ALREADY IN THESE GORGEOUS COLORS.

[opposite, below] I painted some rough stools and benches, which are completely rustic country style. You wouldn't have these in your grand house! These types of stools and benches are made without nails, using traditional woodworking joints.

[right] This interior has a Carl Larsson feel. Larsson, a Swedish painter in the Arts and Crafts tradition, was hugely influential in adding a rustic country feel to Swedish style. He took a folky, "backwards" approach, saying you could look down at the earth and working people for inspiration and ideas, rather than just "up" at royalty-inspired designs and sky blues.

[left] An all-timber interior setting in which the tables, chairs, and table lamps on the porch are made from branches and driftwood. The setting here is in the wilderness of the North American Appalachian mountains.

[opposite] American country-cabin living takes the indoors outside, to give a pared-down, but comfortable and comforting, room setting.

DISTRESSED AND WEATHERED

The rustic style is very much about a weathered and battered look, taking the elements of wind, rain, and sun outside and bringing them back in (the effects, that is, rather than the elements themselves!). It's all about the blurred line between the outside and the inside—indoor furniture can be taken outside but outdoor furniture can also be brought inside. The main image on the opposite page is an excellent example of this, blurring, as well as being a celebration of, log-cabin life and the great outdoors.

Surrounding this picturesque cabin, candles illuminate the twilight and cast a golden glow that radiates warmth and highlights the rough-hewn character of the cabin. It is a humble home with its original wood shingles and siding. Virtually everything is exposed to the elements and naturally weathered: the dining table and bench, with flowers arranged in an enamel pitcher, the wooden chairs and stool, and the rustic seat acting as a side table. The metal rocking chairs are amazingly weathered in their aquamarine and rusty finish. Nearly all the elements

sit on natural timber decking, while the open circular stone fire provides natural heat and light, as well as creating an evocative atmosphere of burning charcoal and wood.

Rustic country's textural effects can be literally those of beds, tables, sideboards, and chairs made from logs, and natural stone fireplaces. Wood, stone, and metal are at its core, and there is a rugged handsomeness about the look, accentuated by the whitewashed finish, earthy colors, and constant usage and worn look of the furniture and accessories.

This style is a celebration of natural and man-made materials that don't need polishing to look immaculate or arranging to look sleek. Exposed brickwork, a passion for wood in its many versatile guises, and using old objects for new purposes are all part of the recipe.

HERE ARE SOME EASILY MADE
PATTERNS THAT WORK WITH RUSTIC
COUNTRY. I PRINTED THESE BY
DIPPING REUSABLE ADHESIVE PUTTY
IN PAINT AND THEN DABBING IT. I
ALSO USED A BIT OF CARD DIPPED IN
PAINT TO CREATE THE LINES. IT
CREATES A NICE, WOBBLY,
TEXTURED EFFECT.

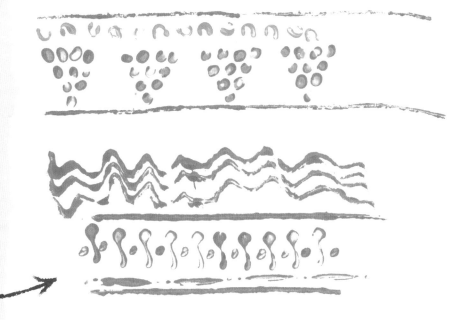

BACK TO BASICS COTTAGE

When we entered this lovely rustic cottage, we were immediately taken with the celebration of the fabric of a home—and that sums up rustic country style. This wonderful abode, owned by Rob and Jane Slater, is located in the rolling hills of the Peak District, in the north of England. Rob and Jane are both collectors and dealers, in their early 50s, and they bought the cottage 16 years ago. They were looking for an "undone-up" place and they certainly found it, here on the edge of a charming market town.

The couple were keen to get a really untouched house, precisely so they could return it to its past. The cottage had been lived in by an old man all his life, and he had done very little to it. It had not been modernized, and nothing had been ripped out. All they had to do was remove some old wallpaper and some modern 1960s shelving. Nothing had been painted, and things had been boarded up rather than stripped out. The house was therefore like a hidden treasure-trove, with its original features waiting to be discovered. Exposing an original Victorian iron range that had not seen the light of day for decades must have felt like the equivalent of unearthing Tutankhamun's tomb for the first time!

The Slaters haven't stripped the cottage back, knocked through walls, replaced the furniture, repainted the interior, and made other improvements. Far from it. They've cleverly drawn out the building's quirkiness, its working roots, its humble origins—and then proudly displayed all its wonderful rustic charms.

FULL OF **CHARACTER**

We entered the cottage via a wonderfully worn and weather-beaten whitewashed timber door, with naturally crackling green paint—the owners have deliberately left this untreated. You couldn't improve on its natural texture or color. The door takes you straight into the kitchen, which is itself a very rustic statement. It's a modest little dwelling, as old working cottages were.

Jane collects spongeware, which is traditional English earthenware originating in the region (see the previous page for some examples). Similar styles are seen all around the world. The cups, saucers, teapots, and other pieces are hand-sponged with decorative patterns (the pigment is dabbed on). The technique was popular in the late 19th century, and the patterns were also spattered on as well as sponged. It has had a renaissance thanks to Emma Bridgewater and other pottery designers. In shorthand, it is very farmhouse and tailor-made for the kitchen setting. The kitchen worktable and sink are original. The tiles, however, were made by Jane at evening classes because she could not find anything in

keeping. Rob went to pottery evening classes too and learned to make a sgraffito type of pottery called slipware. A dedicated couple!

There are very old and uneven flagstones on the floor, which have grooves in them—Rob and Jane think that they might have been for the blood to run along after game had been cut up—but they have been turned over, so the surface is now flat.

[previous page] Jane's collection of spongeware makes an attractive display in the kitchen. We liked the wire-shaped egg basket—it is rustic, utilitarian, and very attractive with the eggs on show.

[opposite] There is a front door but everyone enters the house via this old kitchen door, which is worn and peeling.

[above] The kitchen is chock-a-block with working surfaces, utensils, and tools, in keeping with the rustic character. Everything is on display, within easy reach. Wooden bread and chopping boards are displayed as an ensemble, and there are lots of glass and metal jars. We especially liked the circular rustic rack for hanging pots and pans and other implements.

[left] An old enamel butcher's sign hangs on the wall above some old cast-iron weighing scales. Green is the primary color here, used for the Aga stove and also the wooden, mesh-fronted mini larder. Below is a work surface with a burlap (hessian) floral patterned curtain. Everything is real and old, yet practical and down-to-earth.

[opposite, left] Rob restores everything, scraping off recent layers of paint, to reveal the original workmanship. Sometimes, as with this chair, he just gives the piece a helpful polish or wash, to give it some life.

[opposite, right] The owners try to collect locally, but now and then they buy from all over. They sourced this mini cupboard while on a trip to Romania.

[opposite, below] An iron grappling hook, on which you might hang game to cure, makes an intriguing furnishing in its own right. The wooden spoons displayed proudly in the wooden, open-fronted cabinet are very rustic.

RUSTIC LIVING

The kitchen is the heart of this cottage. Rob and Jane have put in an Aga cast-iron range stove, which is very much in keeping with the working kitchen. A rustic burlap (hessian) curtain conceals the storage area underneath a very rough-and-ready and textural work surface.

The Slaters have always been interested in country pieces, and even on their honeymoon they bought the early farmhouse chair that now takes pride of place in their home. They found it while scouring antique shops and bought it for their house-to-be. The scratched blue is a lovely earthy color, made more alluring by the natural distressed effect. As with so many other pieces of furniture and other smaller accessories that they have purchased, Rob and Jane have done nothing to it and love the way it is worn, even though it is not particularly old.

Rob collects the furniture, and they both attend auctions and fairs all over to search for their pieces. Jane concentrates more on the old English craft of spongeware. The patterns on the earthenware that form her collection are simple and unsophisticated.

MIX ANTIBES GREEN WITH A BIT OF AUBUSSON BLUE TO MAKE A SLIGHTLY DARKER VERSION OF THIS MINI CUPBOARD.

MY DOODLE-LIKE SWIRLS WERE INSPIRED BY THIS COLLECTION OF PRETTY SPONGEWARE. THEY'RE CREATED IN THE SAME WAY AS THE ARTWORKS ON PAGE 157.

HIDDEN TREASURES

As with other parts of the house, the dining area displays a lot of Victorian furniture and furnishings. The absolute knockout centerpiece here is the Victorian cast-iron range, which suggests this was the original kitchen—the range's function would have been cooking as well as heating. When Rob and Jane removed some boarding, they found this hidden gem, uncleaned and unloved, behind it. The textures on it are unbelievable and not just on the cast iron. The wooden surround and mantelpiece are deeply engrained too.

The yellow curtain material is not Jane's first choice but it is an inexpensive substitute for crewelwork. Crewel embroidery is a type of crochet embroidery employed in the 17th century. Jane feels the light-colored fabric works well as drapes since this is quite a dark room. A few strategically placed flowers add to the atmosphere, not least the hyacinths. They provide stunning spring displays, especially in containers, of very fragrant blooms.

[opposite] The dining room curtains are modern but have the look of crewelwork—a 17th-century, Jacobean-style design and one of the earliest forms of surface stitching. Crewelwork tends to be two-tone and uses a range of stitches and elements of shading in crewel wool on linen. Key motifs were insects and quirky animals and foliage designs. The iron pouch for candles and the cylindrical iron candle-holder catch the eye above this cast-iron Victorian range.

[above, left] A welcoming touch is provided by the natural cottage plants, including the hyacinths, on the range. We were smitten by the decoy dove, or pigeon, perched on the side table—so simply created and with the addition of just a little paint.

[above, right] A really lovely, old, oxidized-looking lamp sits beside a still life of a dead hare. In past times, a real hare would have been hung up to cure in the kitchen pantry.

USING TEXTURE

The master bedroom is dominated by an unusual period piece—a heavy oak-panelled bed. The bed is covered by a beautifully embroidered and delicately made antique quilt. The owners ripped off the wallpaper to reveal a very textured and battered wall. They then added a gorgeous and muted mix of whitewash and earthy red. The result is a warm, cozy, and very atmospheric bedroom.

The whole feel here is slightly more upscale than the rest of the cottage, with the pair of gilt-framed still lifes of fruit and the patterned mosaic behind the headboard. The other framed pictures are also slightly "posher" than those displayed elsewhere.

The rustic element in this room comes from the gamekeeper's bag casually hanging from the door; but really it's the texture, texture, and

[above] The bedroom walls are washed in a brown-red, which provides an ideal background for a display of gilt-edged paintings.

[opposite] The stark contrast between the white flowers and terracotta planter and the deep red plastered wall is very effective. It could work just as well if it were an arrangement of, say, red tulips or roses set against uneven white plasterwork.

WHITE FLOWERS, LIKE
THESE, CAN BE SHOWN
TO GOOD EFFECT AGAINST
A BROWN-RED WALL,
ESPECIALLY IF POTTED IN
A SYMPATHETIC TERRACOTTA
"BAKED EARTH" CONTAINER.

yet more texture evident everywhere in this interior, and the very matte, strong red pigment, that define this room. The color is based on an old 19th-century and once ubiquitous pigment called cardinal red. It was a cheap way of painting brickwork and fireplaces and walls, and you saw it everywhere. It's a darker variation of terracotta, literally "fired earth."

Rich brown-reds are very rustic, as they are natural, comforting colors. They go well with other earth pigments, such as yellow ocher and umbers. The Victorians used this brown-red color a lot, especially combined with cream. The pale ceiling, bedroom door, and cupboard door provide ideal neutral finishes to contrast against the

stronger wall color. Warm pinks would have much the same effect, as they are the color of fresh wall plaster and include orange and pale brown shades.

All these variations of red are well suited to the rustic interiors and the vernacular of rustic country. They also go well with wooden floorboards, whether pale pine or heavy oak. The other main complementary color here would be any bluey-green.

BATHROOM **BLUES**

Carrying on upstairs, we came to the small bathroom. Rob and Jane are not sure of the age of the house or the original arrangement of the rooms. They know that the building is mainly 19th century but that some parts could be a lot older and that there were later additions. The bathroom was definitely added because there would not have been one originally, especially upstairs. If there had been a bathtub, it would have been downstairs and most likely in an outhouse.

The bathroom is a mix of blue-green hues and, again, very textured. These colors complement the delightfully rustic Dutch Delft tiles, which show scenes from daily life in 17th-century Holland—Dutch people at work and play. At that time, and into the 18th century, Delft craftsmen successfully imitated Chinese porcelain with their earthenware tiles. Delft blue is known all over the world and is the general name for all earthenware objects and tiles that were painted in this blue color. These tiles were added by the owners and work sympathetically with the rest of the room.

There is some fusing with coastal style in this bathroom, especially with the lighter blue colors used, the painted corner cabinet, and, more obviously, with the simple, almost naive, painting of a local harbor scene with wooden boats. The decoy duck adds a nice, quirky, and watery touch to this wonderful setting.

[above] This rolltop, freestanding, single-ended Victorian bathtub, with its old brass faucets (taps) and ball-and-claw cast-iron feet, is a classic rustic country item. Here it is set in shades of Aubusson Blue and Louis Blue. The chair is a lighter Greek Blue. The natural iron latch on the well-worn door is pure rustic.

[left] This corner cabinet is a practical and attractive piece of furniture in Old Ochre with a Louis Blue surround.

[opposite] This harbor view painting is very rustic and in keeping with the Paris Grey wall and Delft blue tiles. The sponge earthenware on the top shelf sits well next to the forget-me-not plant in an old terracotta pot and the quirky, decoy duck.

paint your own

Aging furniture

This old toolbox has been repainted in earthy reds and blues and now holds all sorts of kitchen bits and pieces. There are many ways paint can be used to age and distress furniture and achieve this look. This piece is already very old and has possibly been painted many times before, so applying another coat of paint will make it look even more textured and worn.

You could try Emperor's Silk, which is scarlet red, or Burgundy, which is a deep cherry color, but I think Primer Red would work best to create a similar rustic effect. It is closest to the original 18th-century artist's pigment and red oxides and ocher reds, which were a reddish-brown.

To create the rustic effect, paint one solid coat of Primer Red on the sides (make sure the surface doesn't have any varnish on it). Leave for an hour. Then rub all over with coarse sandpaper. Vary the pressure as you go for a more textured look. Brush with a clear wax.

Use the same technique for the Aubusson Blue or Napoleonic Blue drawers. If you mix either with a little Primer Red, you will make the blues darker.

[opposite] It's all about the texture, evident here in the very attractively worn cabinet of mini drawers, which was originally a toolbox for keeping nails and other ironware. The distressed paintwork and exposed piping are all part of the look. The traditional wooden candle-holder now contains an assortment of old bone- and wooden-handled carving knives. The metal bull adds a nice rustic touch to this kitchen. Traditional condiments, preserves, and spreads on display provide a range of vintage references too.

[above] I've created this swatch to suggest how you might copy the colors of the cabinet. In it, I've used Primer Red, a deep, warm red, for the sides, and Aubusson Blue, which is a deep blue, for the drawers.

Chapter 8
COASTAL

We love the idea of bringing the seaside into the home. Coastal is bright and breezy, sun-kissed and salty, but it doesn't have to end there. We like to cast our net wider to include moodier, windswept, and wintry inspirations, as well as naval references, not least navy blue.

Coastal colors tend to be washed and faded whites, blues, turquoises, and greens, but you can go bolder and be inspired by the colors of the oceans and tropical seas. Think vivid blues and intense turquoise, as well as the bleaker grays and deep green-blues of the northern seas. Don't forget sandy-colored neutrals and driftwood whites and grays too.

This is a great style for spontaneity. Bring out your inner beachcomber by looking for discarded oyster and scallop shells, sea glass, old rope, driftwood, sand, painted and peeled wood, sea grasses, pebbles, and rocks—these are just some of the many naturally found pieces that will inspire you and help you add a coastal touch to your home.

What's so appealing about coastal is its versatility. It can be combined with maritime culture and seaside resorts, as well as fishing ports and harbors and all their eye-catching imagery. Think nostalgic seaside postcards, vintage naval ephemera, lighthouses, luxury liners, sailing yachts, fishing boats, lobster pots, navigational signage and instruments—just for starters.

Coastal lends itself to plenty of soft furnishings, but it's visually rough-and-ready, reflecting the weathering effect of the wind, sun, and salty air.

[opposite] Homes by the sea have the advantage of reflecting the whites, blues, turquoises, and greens surrounding them, but you can create the coastal look wherever you live.

[above] Colors, especially on fabrics, are fresh, clean, and clear. Here, the starfish hanging on a rope make a perfect coastal reference.

ELEMENTS OF **COASTAL** STYLE

NATURAL FINDS

Nautical, natural, and "found" decor are intrinsic to coastal style. You can't have one without the other. If you live close to the sea, or if you are visiting the seaside, coastal style is perfect for beachcombing and for scooping up the flotsam and jetsam of the shoreline. Found objects, such as fossils and seabird feathers, often work best as nature left them, and the beauty of seashells makes them perfect embellishments or statements in their natural state.

If you are going to display smaller seashells, just empty them randomly into a suitable bowl. If they are quite large and can be displayed individually, pristine seashells will look amazing arranged in a haphazard style—almost chucked away. A more ordered display can look a bit clichéd; if you're not careful, it might start to resemble something found in a seafood restaurant!

If there is one style that is about reacting to your surroundings, then it's coastal. It's about referencing aspects of coastal life in a natural way by reflecting the nature of the shoreline with old seashells, beautifully rounded pebbles, distressed pieces of wood, and other flotsam—old cork buoys, disused fishing nets, and so on. But coastal is also about

nostalgia, about harking back to the heady days of transatlantic luxury liners, a local fishing and shipbuilding industry, bustling ports and harbors, and a world of salty dogs and round-the-world seafarers.

Any stretch of coastline can change dramatically over a few miles, from gentle grass and sand dunes leading onto sandy coves, to sheer chalk cliffs dropping onto cobbled and rocky beaches, to man-made cobs, fashionable beach resorts, and lighthouses, as well as yachting marinas

A WHITEWASHED CLAPBOARD WALL PROVIDES A PERFECT BACKDROP TO AN ECLECTIC MIX OF COASTAL-LINKED OBJECTS, ALONGSIDE THE BRIGHTER WHITE WOODEN CHAIR AND BENCH.

and fishing boats alongside quays. In the same way, you can theme your coastal finds to reflect different aspects of the coastal life.

For a purer, more natural interpretation of the coastline, you can beachcomb for washed-up or discarded items, such as old rope, shells, coral, bits of driftwood (these can look pretty sculptural), old fishing nets, pebbles, dried seaweed, net floats, cork, and so on. These found items look great if given some context and they are, of course, free. If you can't get to the beach, you might find similar finds along inland waterways. Failing that, try stores that sell fishing tackle, souvenirs, and bric-a-brac, as well as ship chandleries.

[opposite, above] Very few objects say coastal so instantaneously as this classic model wooden schooner, next to a starfish.

[above] These various beachcombed and store-bought objects are all coastal style. From top, left to right: pebbles; seashells and wooden peggings for fishing nets; bright turquoise shrimping/rockpool nets, three old floats, and a nautical porthole window. From bottom, left to right: wooden fish carved in a naive style; a natural, distressed fourposter; a collection of old fishing corks, next to a stylized statue of Neptune.

WORKING COASTAL

We find this working theme very appealing. It references the fishing industry, the merchant navy, naval dockyards, longshoremen and stevedores (we love those words), luxury liners, lifeboats and lifeguards, lighthouses, old ferry services, yacht clubs, shipbuilding, even naval warfare, but in a more nostalgic vein, looking back 100 years and beyond.

Vacations by the sea or on the sea also form part of this decor, with vintage postcards or posters of old piers or famous resorts, and retro train, boat, and plane advertisements linking passengers to these destinations. The nostalgia of beach vacations might also include fun fairs, amusement parks, and other forms of pier entertainment that were popular on both sides of the Atlantic. Going back to Victorian times, old black-and-white prints of early seaside frolics, like Punch and Judy shows and donkey rides, are also good ephemera to source.

To some extent, working coastal can overlap with warehouse style (see Chapter 9). You might incorporate artifacts salvaged from ships, such as lamps or portholes, pennants, or old brass instruments used for navigation or measuring water depth or wind and sailing speeds. Other items might include vintage wooden paddles and oars, surfboards, snorkels and masks, old diving gear, fishing tackle, flags, as well as old prints showing seaside towns, harbor views, fishing boats, ships out at sea, and so on.

Look out also for old (or reproduction) posters of the great days of the tea clippers, as well as of the transatlantic and other oceanic passenger liners. Old merchant and military navy prints, and even vintage naval officer uniforms and hats, work very well with natural coastal ephemera too.

Antique stores and markets in coastal locations, as well as ship chandleries and thrift stores, would be good sources for nostalgic coastal ephemera. The great thing about this style is that you don't have to live by the ocean. You could be in a high-rise apartment or country cottage and still easily create a beachy feel.

[top] We love this painting of two boys posing in their naval uniforms. To us, this is archetypal coastal. I bought it in a junk shop in Belgium. The colors and frame are set off nicely against the Aubusson Blue wall. The naval captain in the photo is Felix's grandfather. It makes a great visual connection, along with the other coastal ephemera on the mantelpiece.

[above] This watercolor of a boat out at sea and the classic ship-in-a-bottle have obvious links to the coastal theme.

[right] I like the nautical feel of these lights hanging in wire cages, linked by a pulley system.

[far right] A simply charming, homemade model sailing vessel in Aubusson Blue sits on a piece of distressed wood, alongside a scallop shell. The sails are made from recycled plastic bags. It all looks very natural against the Old White window frame, distressed to look weather-beaten.

THESE SUPERB MODERN TILES ARE DECORATED WITH VINTAGE SEASIDE VACATION SCENES. THE COLORS VEER FROM SANDY YELLOW TO DEEP AZURE. I'VE ALSO SUGGESTED SOME MORE CLASSIC COASTAL COLORS IN THE NAVAL MEDAL RIBBONS BELOW.

COLOR AND TEXTURE

Not surprisingly, a key color of coastal style is the predominant blue of the oceans and seas. Blue is also often the color of the sky, though perhaps a bit more faded at times. Either way, blue is by its nature a cool color, covering a vast range on the color wheel. We also like navy blue, as it creates a more intimate, cozy, and warm feel. Dark shades of blue give a lot of depth and also blend well into the background.

As well as deep-water blues, a coastal palette should include the lighter sea greens and oyster grays for a different watery look. Provence is a greeny-blue and works nicely for all those sea blues. Mix it with Florence for an intense sea green. The turquoises of the Caribbean and the Aegean Seas are very popular, and can be created by mixing Louis Blue or Greek Blue with Old White, while Napoleonic Blue covers the navy blues. Coastal as a color statement also includes a large swathe of muted white, warm gray, and washed-out, earthy ocher, to reflect the sandy pale colors of the beach, as well as the outer hues of shells and the seashore more generally.

Add to this a big touch of distressed paintwork to mimic the weather-beaten look so predominant on seashore esplanades, walkways, and clapboard houses. The idea that the interior has somehow succumbed to years of lashing rain or constant sunshine with the odd storm thrown in is highly appealing—it allows the inclusion in coastal style of very rough paintwork as well as rusty ephemera.

A unified color scheme is a key theme running throughout coastal. Visually, it says smoothness and is soothing—like the feeling of walking barefoot over scrubbed and washed wooden floorboards. However, that doesn't mean you can't add a touch of drama with, say, the red-and-white stripes predominant in lighthouses and sea-channel buoys, or the

[above] Vertical and horizontal wooden boards painted in a distressed Aubusson Blue, together with white window frames, give this garden shed a nautical look.

yellow/red combination seen on beachside flags signifying lifeguards in action. Given that beach style is popular from Scandinavia to the U.S. Eastern Seaboard, the Caribbean, and beyond, the color palette and choice of objects can reference an amazingly varied type of shoreline: cold as well as hot, and darker as well as lighter shades of blue.

The textural element involves heavy distressing to mimic the way the coast is exposed to the elements: The salty air and sea, the high winds,

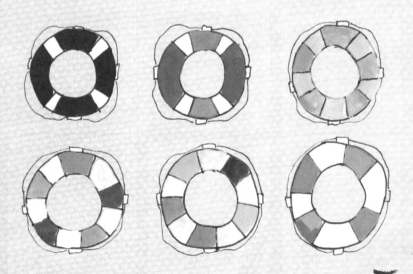

HERE ARE SOME CLASSIC COLOR COMBINATIONS INSPIRED BY DIFFERENT TYPES OF SEASIDE LOCATIONS, WHICH I'VE ILLUSTRATED AS LIFE BUOYS. YOU CAN EXPERIMENT FROM THE ARRESTING RED-AND-WHITE TO THE SOOTHING SANDY COLORS OF PALE YELLOW, GRAYS, AND WHITES.

and the baking sun all accelerate the aging effect, making paintwork peel off and metals rust. Natural materials go hand in hand with coastal, so you will see plenty of exposed timber for floors, walls, and ceilings. Tongue-and-groove wall cladding is popular, as it references yacht cabins, and exposed arched or diagonal rafters add to the airy, "on deck" feel. Tiled floors and rough stone walls, even granite, work well in coastal. Texture is provided by using rattan, sea grass, bamboo, cane, or teak with natural fibers such as linen, sisal, jute, and cottons.

[above] A beautiful, naturally distressed blue door, bordered by rough-hewn and weather-beaten white paintwork, provides a perfect reference for coastal color and texture.

[above] This is my palette of blues, ranging from light grays to ocean blues. For a darker blue, try mixing a bit of Primer Red with Greek Blue, or Aubusson Blue with Barcelona Orange. At the other end of the color wheel, Provence with Old White makes a lovely aquamarine. Louis Blue with Duck Egg Blue and Old White will give you grayer blues.

FISHERMAN'S COTTAGE

This fantastic coastal house tells a story. It is not about sunny seaside vacations, ice creams, and sandcastles, but a local story—that of the working life of a fishing community.

It is owned by Paul Massey, a photographer, and his wife Jules, and located by the quayside overlooking the harbor of an enchanting, tiny, old coastal village on the southern Cornish coast, in the southwest of England. It remains a small, working fishermen's port, supplemented by a huge, seasonal tourist influx.

Many fishermen have worked in this building over several hundred years. It was originally a room on stilts, so that the boats could be stored underneath and the nets laid out to dry in the room above. At some point, walls were added to the boathouse part, and eventually the building was turned into a cottage. It was then occupied by a fisherman and his large sprawling family, who are remembered by many in the village today.

Since buying the house, Paul and Jules have restored it back to its fisherman's roots. They've removed a ceiling, so the old rafters can be seen, and painted everything light, in a limited range of colors, to evoke the open skies and the sea. The whole place has a driftwood look that acknowledges the elements: the sun, wind, and sea spray. It contains some wonderful pieces relating to the local area—much that references the life of the fishermen here.

THE WELCOME OF WASHED WOOD

The house is in the most fabulous, intimate setting, right on the quayside by the fishing boats, but the entrance is at the back, reached through an archway. As we entered, all we could see was painted wood. It felt like we were boarding an old boat, like the inside of an old schooner, although not in an obvious way.

Facing the wooden porch is a white-painted staircase that leads upstairs to the sitting room and kitchen. (The bathroom and the two bedrooms and study are downstairs.)

The upstairs sitting room is at the front of the house, and has magnificent views overlooking the harbor. It was absolutely wonderful to just sit and watch the activity of fishing boats and other vessels coming in and out of the harbor entrance.

[previous page] This upper-floor room was designed for storing fishing nets. It is the exact dimensions as the nets were, with a high, vaulted ceiling that allowed space for them to hang. The ceiling was put in when the building was made into a cottage, but later removed by Paul and Jules when they restored it to its fishing roots.

[opposite] The collections of found objects around the house give a multitextured feel against the weathered, washed-out wooden wall. The map of Cornwall, the old black-and-white framed print and postcard, the driftwood, and the pebbles all reflect a love of the locality.

[above] A passion for nature is displayed on this tabletop, with a swallow print, sea anenome, shells, pebbles, and nature book among the array of natural objects.

In this corner of Cornwall you are very aware of the weather through all the seasons, and it's reflected in the house, in particular in this room. The floor is all wood and washed with a gray-white paint, and this effect is continued up the end wall, giving the feeling of being inside the wooden cabin of a large yacht.

The room is also reminiscent of driftwood, that is wood that has been bleached by the elements and seawater. Accordingly, the color palette of this house is very narrow indeed—a small range of neutrals from off-white to light charcoal gray, with light gray and very light brown. Everything is in keeping—the washed wood, the chipped and worn paintwork of the tabletops, the exposed chopped logs for the wood burner. To ensure that these few colors remain interesting, they are differentiated by the use of many textures and materials. Nearly everything has a matte finish but the textures vary from knobbly to plain, with smooth old white papers on maps and book covers, and grayed woods with a gentle grain, for instance.

There are a few shiny pieces dotted here and there, such as the metal lamp stand and silver saucer, as well as the glass jars and the gentle sheen on some of the shells—a little sheen cleverly highlights the matte finish of the room.

NATURAL LINENS AND CANVAS ADD
SOME BASIC COMFORT TO AN OTHERWISE
STRIPPED-BACK CORNER. THE SALVAGED
SEARCHLIGHT, WITH THE "THROWAWAY"
BINOCULARS, ADDS A TOUCH OF
"LIGHTHOUSE LOOKOUT," WHILE THE OLD
CHEST IS PERFECT FOR STORING BOOKS.

[opposite] Although this birdhouse is not strictly a coastal object, it is
reminiscent of the kind of wooden hut you might expect to find down by
the shore, and its highly distressed finish fits in perfectly with the style.
The weather-ravaged wood and pale paintwork have just the right kinds
of textures for the coastal look.

[right] The large wooden model schooner suggests a bygone era of classic
yachting without being clichéd. Old sponges, a shutter, and other found
objects reinforce the seafaring imagery.

The kitchen is also upstairs, in a new extension next to the living room, which it mirrors in size and in terms of being "exposed." It, too, has weather-beaten wooden beams and exposed roof rafters. Like the living room, it is very light and airy, and the color palette is similar. However, it sits on the industrial warehouse spectrum of coastal style—far removed from seaside shells and driftwood, or the coastal style of nostalgic naval ephemera.

The cross reference between coastal and warehouse comes from the salvaged elements—especially the metal pendant lampshades with chain hangings—and the distressed paintwork on wood surfaces. This room also reinforces the important point that when it comes to choosing a style, you don't have to hammer it home in every single room. There is always room for the exception that (perhaps) proves the rule.

HARBORSIDE LIVING

We headed back downstairs to the bedrooms via an enclosed staircase, which is reminiscent of a schooner; the owners have heightened this feel by hanging several lamps that we could imagine being used on a fishing boat at night. A porthole would not have been out of place, but there is nothing obvious in this house.

The references to the sea are not direct or clichéd. Both bedrooms look out directly onto the harbor front, so that the windows are like frames to postcard views, and because they are at ground level, you feel an immediacy with the outside—the fishing boats and the old stone capstans on the harbor edge. The windows are set deep and are cottage-sized, with large wooden sills, painted in the distressed style, perfect for displaying found objects. There are no curtains, just white roller blinds, which add to the no-frills, workmanlike feel.

These rooms are very minimal and calm and are similarly styled as the sitting room. The bedroom with the two windows is the main bedroom, and the other room, with one window and a large armoire, is used as a dressing room or for guests. The overall impression is of white, with clear sea light coming from the deep cottage windows.

[previous page, left] This salvaged depth gauge, used for measuring and indicating water levels, is one of the many workmanlike pieces collected by Paul and Jules. These gauges are often seen at harbor entrances or attached to channel buoys as a tide and depth indicator, as well as at river and canal locks and weirs.

[previous page, right] The kitchen displays a light sheen with the polished white floor and wall tiles. A little sheen goes a long way to offsetting the dominance of the overall matte finish still evident in the wooden ceiling and rafters, and the furniture. The kitchen is housed in a new extension and displays the industrial "warehouse" side of coastal style with the white, fishmonger-style tiles and metal pendant ceiling lights.

[opposite] The kitchen cabinet displays a carefully curated collection of plates, cups, saucers, egg cups, and other artifacts, all enhancing the washed-out and airy whites, grays, and blues of the room's interior.

[above] This corner of the kitchen is dominated by off-white, weather-beaten wooden walls, rafters and shelving, set off by the black metal industrial pendant lamps and deep blue coffee mugs, for added color.

Overall, this incredible house displays beautifully worn and weather-battered interiors that are a classic take on matte and subdued coastal style, where nothing is too precious—shells can be handled, furniture snuggled into, and drawers opened. The shelves display nautical ephemera, natural elements, and no hint of florals.

The muted palette and matte finish both work extremely well to give a unified color scheme that exudes a sense of relaxed informality and unpretentiousness. The colors create a sense of relaxed informality and unpretentiousness, which is enhanced by the decorative accessories.

The coastal theme is reinforced by the natural material of the pillows and bedding, as well as by all the decorative elements. Note the exposed and scrubbed granite pillar in the bedroom (overleaf)—a natural material next to natural, stripped-back, and washed wooden floorboards—and the simple storage all around—exactly what you would expect on board a ship.

[above] The distressed coat rack has been sanded back and painted in an Aubusson Blue mix to mimic the driftwood you might find on a beach battered by the elements.

[opposite, above] The knotted rope key fob has an eye-catching nautical reference, while the brass wall light has been salvaged from an old boat cabin. Light-reflecting materials such as glass and mirror play an important role in coastal style.

[opposite, below] Not all objects in a room have to slavishly reference a nautical theme; the horse, for example, might be just a loose link with horses galloping in the sand. The ammonite directly references a Jurassic shoreline, while the brass compass-holder protects an old-fashioned swivel compass once used on a sailing yacht. The old metal lobster pot over a bowl of sea anemones makes an eye-catching window shelf display.

[overleaf, left] The bathroom echoes the classic coastal feel in its color palette (notice the gray side of the tub) and textures, with the wood paneling and the distressed wood cabinet supporting the stylish sink.

[overleaf, right] The bedroom is all about the textural feel of smooth and rough linens, while the bed's wooden drawer echoes a bunkbed on board a smart yacht. The white-bordered map of Cornwall and the Scilly Isles pays direct tribute to the house's location.

paint your own

Distressed paintwork

A strong feature of seaside towns and villages is the way that any exterior paintwork is quickly worn and distressed by salty winds and sea spray. If you can't find pieces of furniture or accessories with old paintwork, then try creating the look yourself.

It is best to use old wood, preferably something that is uneven and textured from having been outside for a long period of time. New paintwork on old wood distresses really well if you want a good, worn, characterful finish.

The bench (opposite) is an old, rough, wooden one with gray, distressed paintwork. To achieve a similar-looking piece, you need to find furniture that is made from relatively rough, uneven wood.

Apply the paint and then, before waxing it, sand it gently with medium to rough sandpaper, to take the paint off in large swathes. Take care not to scratch the paint. When you are finished, apply a clear wax.

The material for the cushion—a very coastal look—is a coarse, vintage French linen and can be used for traditional toweling.

[above] Blues and greens contrast nicely when freshly painted on natural wood, and are suggested alternatives to the colored bench (opposite) and mirror (top). Remember that each piece of old or found wood has its own unique properties and will react differently to the same paint color or technique.

Chapter 9

WAREHOUSE

There's something about warehouse living that brings out the artist in both of us. Perhaps it's because this style started with artists, designers, writers, and printmakers moving to storage and factory lofts in New York and London in the late 1960s.

We love the stripped-back, exposed nature of warehouse interiors. This is rough love, rough luxe: battered is good. You wouldn't call this style cute or charming. It's functional—an all-purpose framework where the simplicity of the furnishings concentrates your eye on the form. It's versatile. It can be mixed nicely with modern retro and coastal styles.

Warehouse is made up of salvaged and upcycled functional furniture and ornaments, giving items such as crates, signage, rubber flooring, and metal lighting a new twist. The style developed from people looking to nonresidential buildings for living space and from designers being inspired by workplace settings. As designers and architects started to create far more cutting-edge interiors in the workplace, people wanted the same look at home. For example, the anglepoise lamp and the venetian blind have migrated to the modern living space. Both are completely functional and "industrial," and are now icons for home use.

Although the desire to collect and celebrate industrial items is a modern trend, it is still looking back (this time to an industrial, pre-computer era), just as neoclassical looks back to a classical age.

[opposite] This industrial catering cart has been adapted with solid wood trays to make an eye-catching shelving unit. The stackable studio stools come from Tolix, a French manufacturer of galvanized sheet-metal domestic items since the 1930s.

[above] The rope, wood, leather, metal, and concrete materials shown here are very much warehouse style. The crate is a functional object that can be used as a side table or coffee table. Resting on top is an altometer (surveying instrument) we salvaged for its aesthetic appeal. Beside the crate is a leather Gladstone bag.

ELEMENTS OF **WAREHOUSE** STYLE

INDUSTRIAL FURNITURE AND LIGHTING

The attraction of industrial furniture is its simplicity and the fact that it is totally functional—think of the metallic ceiling lamps spreading diffused light in fashionable clothes stores. The beauty is in the form and function, and the basic materials used to create these essentials, which are structural in design, look solid (even if they aren't), and are built to be bashed about a bit!

Warehouse items look distressed because they have lived a life in the office or factory already. They have served their time and function. Of course, as this style becomes more popular, reproductions come on the market. Now many "warehouse" pieces, such as industrial furniture, are brand-new and sold in specialist shops and home-interior stores. Some of this modern-made furniture is given a "distressed" look, as if it has just come out of a warehouse.

[above] We adapted these two wooden boxes by fitting them with casters. A bottle box is now a magazine rack, and a wine crate becomes a wine rack.

[left] This Plexiglas (Perspex) bowl contains an unplanted bulb, which is starting to sprout, sitting on top of moss—an indication of the sort of planting that will work in warehouse style. The roots are on display, just like exposed pipework or brickwork. We thought this was a lovely, poetic response to the exposed elements. It is what it is.

A simple way to create an "industrial look" is by sourcing virtually any old storage unit and putting it on casters. The wheels can be bought from DIY stores. Warehouse furniture and furnishings tend to have exposed fixings, so the bolts and the screws will be visible. Butterfly nuts will poke out of a lamp fitting, for instance, rather than be tucked away, and if you have exposed pipework, especially metallic, you don't cover it up—you flaunt it and rejoice in its functionality.

The same principle applies to indoor plants—big, structural plants work particularly well in this environment—a whole gnarled branch covered in moss, for instance. Pretty, arranged

THIS CLASSIC BACKSTAGE THEATER LIGHT IS A GOOD EXAMPLE OF HOW WAREHOUSE STYLE REPURPOSES AND ADAPTS A FUNCTIONAL ITEM FOR DOMESTIC USE.

flowers are not going to impact so forcefully because you're not really putting decorative elements into the warehouse style. It is the structural element itself that is decorative—the trunk, the leaf, or the roots. Think pussy willow, a magnolia branch, or a New Zealand fern.

Lighting salvaged from old offices, stores, and factories is functional and has an appealing simplicity in its forms and shapes. A typical piece is the metallic pendant shade hanging from the ceiling with the cord intertwined and supported by a hard-wearing metal chain. Again, many outlets sell enamel or tinned pendant reproductions of the originals.

Another great example of industrial lighting can be seen on page 177, in the Coastal chapter. There, the pendant lights, hanging from a chain, are referencing the fishing industry.

[right] A loudspeaker becomes a fully functioning lampshade. The Edison bulb is often seen in warehouse style. It has a very dim light and a beautiful filament—it is easy to admire the craftsmanship.

NATURAL MATERIALS AND TEXTURES

Warehouse materials are those of the Industrial Revolution: the factory floor, the concrete surfaces, the exposed metal window surrounds, lighting units, leather fittings, as well as wooden storage and other units. Because warehouse style is in a sense anti-decorative, you are more reliant on the natural materials and textures that make up the framework of the interior. This will include exposed architectural features such as concrete, brick, bare wood from floorboards and beams, and exposed metalwork such as metal beams and steel girders. The effect is also heightened by the fact that warehouse and loft living tends to be open-plan, often with the walls, flooring, and ceiling materials and textures running through the whole interior.

There are also man-made materials such as compressed paper or cardboard, burlap (hessian), and rubber. You can try a mixture of matte and shiny, smooth and rough. Metal, for instance, can be polished and shiny, which will contrast with some of the rougher textures.

[opposite] The exposed brick wall shows previous layers of plaster and paint that have been peeled back, creating a highly textured effect. The exposed metalwork of the shower and the wall lamp celebrates the engineering of both utilities and harks back to an industrial era.

[above] From top, left to right: washed wood on a cart with a rope handle and painted inner tray; a vintage ski boot— we love the leather and the metal studs; an enamel wall advertisement that has rusted, exposing the base metal beneath. From bottom, left to right: a painted, washed, and distressed concrete floor; pressed cardboard numbers; a French burlap (hessian) sack from a flour mill.

DISTRESSED PAINTWORK

Part of the challenge—and fun—of warehouse is scouring local stores, reclamation yards, even dumpsters (skips), to find already distressed doors, panels, and other decor pieces. If you need to extend a naturally distressed piece of paneling, try sourcing or buying something that is new or unblemished and then painting, waxing, and sanding it for that distressed look. If you are going to do this yourself, you will need to paint the furniture first, before sanding it down with rough sandpaper and waxing it. To create a more hardworking and well-worn look, we sand before waxing to reveal the contours and previous finishes of the wood. (Normally you would wax before sanding.)

Do the paintwork in different directions and thicknesses over a first coat, so you can chip it off and make it look really "chipped" and cracked. This could even be four coats to achieve a particular chipped look. Sand the areas you want to look chipped quite hard. Before the second coat is completely dry, you can brush another layer of clear wax over the piece using a clean, dry cloth to get that distressed paintwork look. Printing with corrugated card is a neat way to achieve the distressed look because it produces quite rough textures. Remember that you are looking for a weathered and well-used, not delicate, finish, and that a piece going into a warehouse style has had a hard life and been battered about and somewhat mistreated.

With warehouse style you get very little color throughout. Blues and grays dominate, and tonally it is quite dark. You are relying mainly on natural materials for color, and the only warm colors come from the bricks, with a little warmth from wood. When you are dealing with a very limited color palette, you have to get variation through texture.

[above] An arrangement of new and reclaimed wooden doors, showing a visually sympathetic gradation of distressed effects. This is enhanced by the clever mix of colors and paint effects. The "texture" palette can be as rough-and-ready as you want to make it.

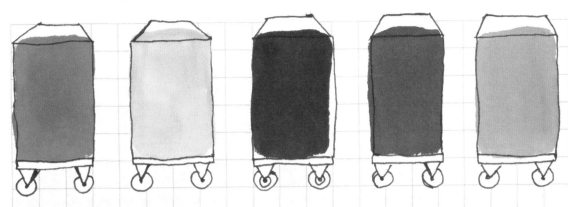

HERE ARE "CART" SWATCHES OF THE PREDOMINANT WAREHOUSE COLORS. FROM LEFT TO RIGHT: FRENCH LINEN, ENGLISH YELLOW, GRAPHITE, EMPEROR'S SILK, AND PARIS GREY. THE YELLOW AND GRAPHITE ARE HIGH-VISIBILITY COLORS, MIMICKING THE YELLOW-BLACK CHEVRON STRIPES TYPICAL OF INDUSTRIAL WARNING SIGNS. COLORS TEND TO BE PRIMARY—PAINT IT YELLOW, PAINT IT RED, SO EVERYONE CAN SEE IT. THE MUTED AND EARTHY FRENCH LINEN AND GRAY MIMIC THE NATURAL TEXTURES OF STONE, CONCRETE, AND WOOD.

[above and right] One way to get the look of old furniture is to use corrugated card to print texture. I've created a browny-red using Primer Red and Emperor's Silk (above), and then applied graphite paint to some corrugated card and printed it. The result is this uneven but regulated look, which is very warehouse. This room features an old door (right) in which paint has been worked through on the panels (as you might find in a studio or warehouse). The workshop feel is made more obvious by the battered and splattered wooden filing chest with brass handles.

AN AMSTERDAM WAREHOUSE

We entered this stunning apartment from the brick-cobbled street through the huge, old, original front door, and the warehouse feeling was with us straightaway. The building is located in the Jordaan area of old Amsterdam, along a narrow street filled with a mixture of workshops, studios, and homes.

Emily Gray and her family live here. She manages to combine domestic life with a home-run organic childrenswear business very well, in a stylish, modern living space that works effectively as a home and an office.

Old Amsterdam was a mass of canals, where goods from around the world were brought in on barges, stored, traded, and transported onward. Nowadays, a lot of these old warehouses, many dating from the 17th century, have been remodeled into engaging and stylish residences. Thankfully, most have kept and enhanced the essence of their industrial working roots.

The entranceway in this apartment houses the family's wonderful, sturdy Dutch bicycles. It is essential for every Amsterdam residence to make space for this number one mode of transport.

IN A BREAK FROM THE EXPANSE OF RED, THERE IS AN AREA WHERE THE BRICKWORK HAS A WHITEWASH (SEE PAGE 154) OVER IT. THIS BRINGS THE WALL CLOSER IN HUE TO OTHER SURFACES AROUND IT: THE BLUE-GRAY COLORED CONCRETE AND THE WELL-USED VINTAGE CHOPPING BOARDS.

OPEN-PLAN LIVING

The living area is one very large open-plan room. The kitchen, dining, sitting, and play areas all flow from one to another on the same level, with the same dark gray concrete flooring throughout.

The only architectural change between each zone is the ceiling height. The kitchen area has a very high ceiling, and there is a large skylight through which natural light enters the apartment. Light also streams into a small courtyard, where there are several large dramatic-looking New Zealand tree ferns, and through the floor-to-ceiling windows into the living area.

One of the many visually stunning points about this apartment is the huge, old brick wall of the kitchen and the courtyard, which runs through from the entranceway. It tells a little of the story of what was here before, with paler-colored old painted bricks and notches suggesting a different roof shape and old rafters. It also provides the strongest color in the whole space—a delightful, warm, mottled terracotta red.

The focus of the room is the spectacular, large wooden chandelier hung from a factory pulley on a rope. This is in sharp contrast to the rest of the apartment for being absolutely opposite to the warehouse style, but its outsized curvy shape, the color, and the matte texture make it the perfect matching, yet contrasting, piece for the room.

[previous page] A range of different materials and textures are celebrated in the dining area with the mixture of outdoor furniture (the wooden bench and dining table) and indoor furniture (the leather and cloth-covered chairs). In contrast to the rough-and-ready finishes, the African chandelier adds a twist of ironic decadence. That dramatic playfulness is carried on with the oversized silverware hanging on the wall.

[opposite] In keeping with the muted, natural color palette and natural finishes, the bar is covered in stitched brown leather. The trio of French 1950s studio stools add steel to the repertoire of materials. A conventional flower arrangement would look out of place in the warehouse setting, so Emily has opted to fill her countertop vase with pussy willow and a magnolia branch. They stand proud as architectural statements: big and bold, rather than delicate and pretty.

[overleaf, left] As well as the working extractor fan above the stove, there is an additional hood and chimney pipe at the end of the counter. In a warehouse setting, this does not look at all out of place. Exposed pipes only add to the industrial feel.

[overleaf, right] The washroom continues the outdoor theme with its big stone backsplash and basin set against rugged old scaffolding boards. A 19th-century brass faucet (tap) adds another raw material to the functional but intimate setup.

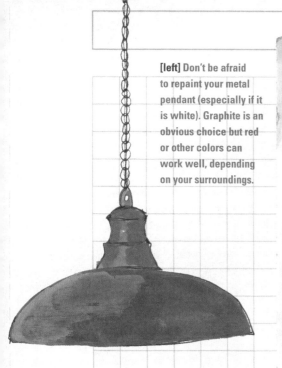

[left] Don't be afraid to repaint your metal pendant (especially if it is white). Graphite is an obvious choice but red or other colors can work well, depending on your surroundings.

A KITE MADE IN THE SHAPE OF A SAILING SHIP, ALONG WITH THE WOODEN BIRDHOUSES, ADDS A LIGHT TOUCH TO THIS EXPOSED BRICKWORK. THE MUTED COLOR PALETTE ALSO CONTRIBUTES TO THE WAREHOUSE FEEL.

BOLD STATEMENTS

With an open, architectural design that is inspired by, and draws from, the basic warehouse space, a large, bold style for the interior decoration and design is necessary, rather than something that is conservative and traditional. The building's industrial history is accentuated by working with its height and stripping the space back to the essential structure. The design style is mainly inspired by warehouse and loft living, but it is done in a personal way with the inclusion of some romantic pieces, such as the chandelier (see page 205) and the armoire (see overleaf).

Emily works from home, a task that people often relegate to a room at the top of the house or to a shed in the garden, but here it takes center stage. It is the first room you come to after parking your bike in the entranceway. There is a large table, computers, office files, and a phone. Although this working area is separate from the other areas of the apartment, it still shares the limelight.

There is a small space like an inner lobby between the office entrance and the main living area, where there is a downstairs cloakroom and a second, small kitchen. Entering the main living space to your left is the other kitchen, which takes up a long galley shape in the room, with a long bar counter helping to conceal the sink and dishwasher.

As the apartment is largely open-plan, the design and colors need to work together. The architecture of the apartment means that the style and palette upstairs have to work with the rest of the house—the bedrooms overlook the kitchen and courtyard.

Through huge windows a small outside courtyard can be seen, which allows fresh air and alfresco dining, but largely the whole apartment is one large play area, as the floors are uncarpeted. The children are free to ride their bicycles and scooters and even kick a soft ball. Part of the warehouse style in this case is to integrate hardy garden furniture into the interior, as well as items that might have been used in factories and designers' studios.

[opposite] Bikes are essential to the Amsterdam way of life and the added internal glass wall in the entranceway celebrates their functionality. This is an example of bringing the outdoors indoors.

CITY LIVING

Emily has cleverly achieved a stylish look to the apartment, despite living with young children in a relatively small space. Living in a city means having few outside areas in which to play, but this apartment uses appropriate, robust building materials in large rooms, which allow the children to run around safely and enjoy rough-and-tumble play.

It's clear that children live in this apartment, but the toys don't create a mess or clutter. To balance the jumble of stylish playthings, Emily has used a large and dominating piece of furniture: her grand and beautiful French armoire. A dark painted wall may not be everyone's preferred backdrop to a child's room but it sets everything off and makes the space smart and elegant.

The boy's room has large windows with a door, which lead to the balcony and overlook the kitchen, so there is plenty of light. The cheerful collection of interesting and amusing objects makes this room magical and charming: the reds and blues of the toys, such as the pirate ship; the graphic shape of the star; the teddy bear; and the star-shape pattern on the duvet. The child's name is Beer, hence the Bs and the name on the wall ("beer" is Dutch for "bear" and nothing to do with the drink!).

THE CABINET IS PAINTED PARIS GREY WITH OLD WHITE. MY COLOR PALETTE BELOW SHOWS SOME ALTERNATIVES THAT FIT THE WAREHOUSE STYLE. THESE ARE, FROM LEFT TO RIGHT: ENGLISH YELLOW, EMPEROR'S SILK, AND PROVENCE (ALL WITH A SMALL, DRY BRUSHING OF GRAPHITE ADDED AND WAXING).

[opposite] Although stylistically this beautiful, decorative 19th-century armoire is in contrast to the industrial setting, the color of the wood is very appropriate. The collection of butterflies works alongside the armoire, continuing the 19th-century look. The bikes, tricycles, and scooters are a clue to modern Amsterdam living.

[above] Although the contents of this child's bedroom are not strictly speaking "warehouse," they do adhere to the color palette seen throughout the rest of the apartment. Mixed into the muted grays and blues are natural, earthy-brown tones, with bright, primary-red highlights adding powerful accents. The use of children's toys as ornaments adds to the sense of fun.

LIGHT AND NATURAL

The bedrooms don't strictly adhere to the warehouse style, but they do work with the rest of the apartment. Emily has achieved this by using similar colors and natural fabrics, such as cottons and linens for the curtains and beds, with light wooden floors throughout.

The bedrooms overlook the courtyard and the main living area, adding to the open-plan feel, with a balcony walkway overlooking the kitchen area. Their large, floor-to-ceiling windows fill the room with light from the courtyard skylight. The red brick wall is again ever-present and provides a strong unifying color for the rooms upstairs.

The comfortable, romantic master bedroom overlooks the courtyard, so that the bed has views of large, tropical-looking tree ferns. These, combined with the safari-type bed canopy, manage to transport you somewhere rather exotic, possibly Indonesia or Africa, rather than a city in northern Europe.

This apartment has terrific architecture, which is what makes the space so exciting. Little needs to be changed because it is so inspiring. However, the decoration has been done in a way that softens and makes the space romantic and very appealing.

[opposite] These vintage children's toys suit the warehouse style because of their natural color palette and exposed wood finish.

[above, right] Making a home of an old warehouse is essentially architectural repurposing, so quirks will always be inherited in the process. In this apartment, one such quirk is this door leading to a void, where you would expect to have just a window.

[right] The canopy above the bed is reminiscent of the kind of outdoor canopy you would expect to find on an African safari, with twig-inspired metal lamp bases on the bedside tables. Maintaining the affair with unadorned natural materials, the bed is dressed with plain white linens and cottons.

Weathered wood

What appears to be rough wooden planking is, in fact, a set of large drawers, holding all the kitchen utensils, equipment, and dry foods. The wood is old and weathered after being left upright outside for a few years to bring out any movement and to help discoloration. Large rough knots and the open gnarled grain of the wood are on clear display.

Look for old wood by visiting salvage yards. Elm and oak work particularly well. Finding the right texture is not easy and the color may not be the one you want, but it can be adjusted.

Coloring wood to allow the grain to show through can be done in two ways and depends largely on the original color and state. One method is to dilute Paris Grey with water—start with a 60 percent paint/40 percent water mix. Apply with a brush and wipe with a cloth as you go. This method is more of a stain than the second method and allows not only the grain to show up well but also the nuances of the original aged wood. Apply wax or a matte varnish for protection.

Alternatively, apply the paint undiluted then allow it to dry. Immediately take a damp sponge or cloth and softly wipe the paint. Leaving it too long means the paint hardens, making it more difficult to remove. Use a dry cloth to adjust the patina you are making as you go. This method will leave stronger and larger areas of gray, rather than mainly translucent paint.

[opposite] Natural white wood painted with a yellow stain.

[above] My swatch suggests four other different stains of color you can add to rough wood to show up the grain and make a big difference to the original color. Here, I've painted Graphite, Greek Blue, Country Grey, and Pure. Be prepared to experiment because what works with one piece of old wood probably won't work with another, as each piece will have its own natural qualities.

THE CHALK PAINT® RANGE

My purpose-made paint, Chalk Paint®, will enable you to achieve the paint techniques described in this book. To understand how color works, use the color wheel, opposite, which not only shows the paint available in the range, but also how they sit together. Next to the color wheel you will find my neutrals, too.

Understanding the color wheel

Mixing and combining paint is easily done if you know how color works, and for this a color wheel can be helpful. I have made my own using my paint colors. As you can see, there aren't a huge number of paints in my range. That's because by simply making them paler, darker, warmer, or cooler, it's possible to create an infinite number of colors.

The color wheel can be used in several ways:
• To darken a color—I rarely use black to make a color darker but, instead, add a complementary color, so the result is more stimulating, complex, and interesting.
• To find a color that will work next to or underneath another color.
• To make a color warmer or cooler.
• For inspiration!

The triangle of colors indicates the three primary colors, which can't be mixed from other colors. Mix red and yellow together to make orange, mix yellow and blue together to make green, and mix blue and red together to make purple. I have placed my colors around this triangle of colors to show, for instance, that Old Violet is nearer to the blues than Emile.

Finding a color's complementary color, such as with the painted drawers in Modern Retro (see page 78) is simply a case of looking at the other side of the wheel at its "opposite" color. Facing English Yellow, for example, is Emile. Use a little Emile to darken English Yellow or use the two colors together, but alter their tonal values by adding Old White. If you want clashing colors, such as in the Bohemian look (see Chapter 4), use adjacent primary and secondary colors, such as Emperor's Silk and Emile or Old Violet, or Emperor's Silk and Barcelona Orange.

Using neutrals

Neutral colors are essential to any room. You can use a lot of strong, bright colors in a room as long as you use lots of white too. Use Pure for a more modern look and Old White or Original for a more mellow or older

neutrals

Pure

Paris Grey

Original

French Linen

Old White

Graphite

look. If you want a more intense color, use some Graphite next to it and notice how it will appear brighter. If you want to soften a color, use one of the grays. These have been inspired by mixing complementaries, then adding white. Paris Grey, for instance, is Barcelona Orange and Greek Blue. French Linen is a color which is a perfect, cool neutral, neither dark nor light. It works with more or less everything.

Stockists

Chalk Paint® is available throughout the UK, Europe, Canada, US, South Africa, Japan, Australia, and New Zealand. For a complete list of stockists where you can buy Chalk Paint® and my other products, please go to www.anniesloan.com.

Please note that the swatches shown here are only a representation of the paints. If ordering, please send your name and address to anniesloancolourcards@gmail.com for a hand-painted color card (UK only). Each color card contains our entire range of colors.

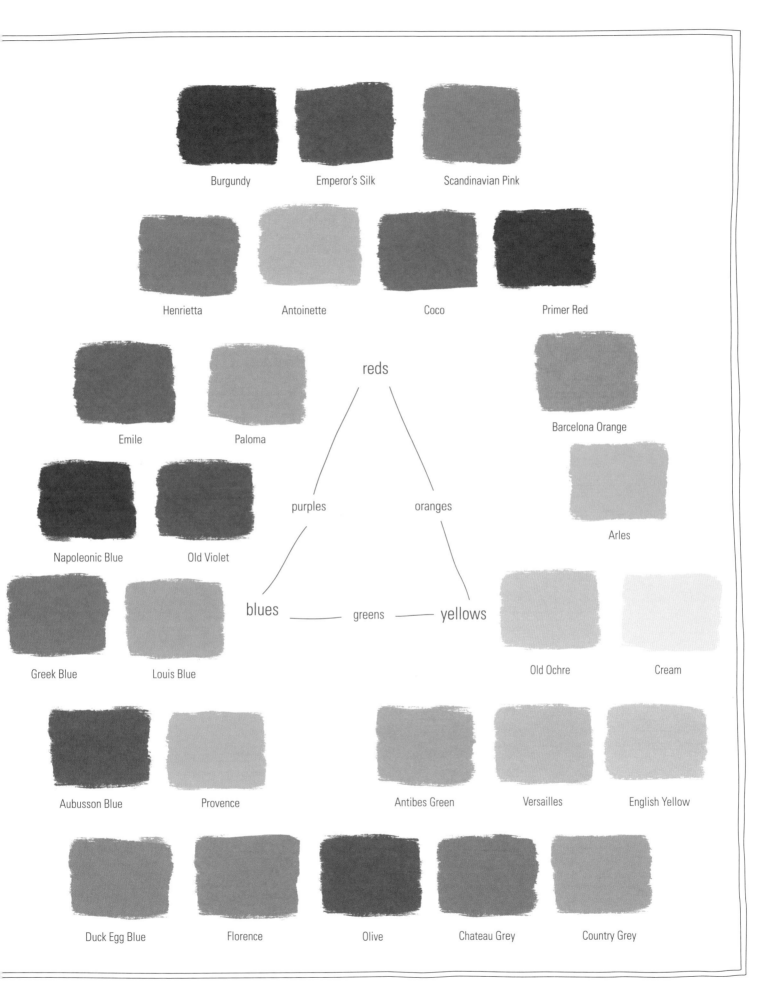

Burgundy

Emperor's Silk

Scandinavian Pink

Henrietta

Antoinette

Coco

Primer Red

Emile

Paloma

reds

Barcelona Orange

Napoleonic Blue

Old Violet

purples

oranges

Arles

Greek Blue

Louis Blue

blues

greens

yellows

Old Ochre

Cream

Aubusson Blue

Provence

Antibes Green

Versailles

English Yellow

Duck Egg Blue

Florence

Olive

Chateau Grey

Country Grey

BUSINESS CREDITS

LOCATION OWNERS

Virginia Armstrong
www.roddyandginger.co.uk
Pages 6ar, 9a, 63a, 64b, 68–79

Alex Russell Flint
www.alexrussellflint.com
Pages 3, 7al, 126–127, 133r,
134–149

Gosling Ltd
Sycamore House
4 Old Town
London SW4 0JY
T: +44 (0)20 7498 8335
E: info@tgosling.com
www.tgosling.com
Pages 17, 20l/c/r, 24–37

Emily Gray
Oude looiersstraat 51
1016 VG Amsterdam
E: info@gray-label.com
www.gray-label.com
http://flow.nu
Pages 13, 198b, 204–215

Janice Issitt
Can be found on Twitter
Facebook: Janice Issitt Life & Style
Blog:
janiceissittlifestyleblogspot.co.uk
Pages 81, 88–101, 107b, 109l/r

Paul Massey, Photographer
www.paulmassey.me
Pages 11, 180–195

Rob and Jane Slater
Decorative Antiques
E: rjs53@btinternet.com
Pages 12a, 158–171, 174b,
175ar/br, 178

Stola Herrgård
Strö 531, 98 Lidköping, Sweden
T: +46 (0)510180 30
E: stola@lidkoping.se
www.stola.se
Pages 6c/bl, 40a/b, 42–44
.(except 42b), 46–59

Madeline Tomlinson of
Weathered and Worn
High Street
Hadlow
Tonbridge
Kent TN11 0EF
E: Madeline@weatheredandworn.me
www.weatheredandworn.me
Pages 1, 7ar, 103, 110–125

FEATURED DESIGNERS

Lubna Chowdhary
www.lubnachowdhary.co.uk
Designer of the ceramic tile panel on
pages 63 and 79

One Must Dash
www.onemustdash.com
Designers of the "Smalltalk" poster
on page 79

Skinny laMinx
www.skinnylaminx.com
Designer of the "tall pincushion"
pillow on page 70 (far right)

Studio Snowpuppe
www.studiosnowpuppe.nl
Designers of the "Moth" lampshade
on page 76

PICTURE CREDITS

Key: a = above; b = below; l = left; c = center; r = right; ph = photographer.

Where not otherwise stated, photography is by Christopher Drake.

Page 1 The home of Madeline Tomlinson of Weathered and Worn.
Page 3 The French home of artist Alex Russell Flint.
Page 4 The home of photographer and interior decorator Janice Issitt.
Page 6ar The home of the designer Virginia Armstrong of
www.roddyandginger.co.uk.
Page 6c/bl Stola Herrgård, Sweden www.stola.se.
Page 7al The French home of artist Alex Russell Flint.
Page 7ar The home of Madeline Tomlinson of Weathered and Worn.
Page 8 Ph: Andrew Wood.
Page 9a The home of the designer Virginia Armstrong of
www.roddyandginger.co.uk.
Page 11 The home of the photographer Paul Massey in Cornwall.
Page 12a The family home of Rob and Jane Slater, Derbyshire.
Page 13 The family home of the designer Emily Gray of www.gray-label.com.
Page 14 The home of Marina Coriasco. Ph: Polly Wreford.
Page 16 Ph: Simon Brown.
Page 17 The home of the designer Tim Gosling in London.
Page 20l/c/r The home of the designer Tim Gosling in London.
Page 22 Ph: Simon Brown.
Page 23a Ph: Andrew Wood; 23b Ph: Simon Brown.
Pages 24–37 The home of the designer Tim Gosling in London.
Page 38 The London home of Shane Meredith and Victoria Davar of Maison
Artefact. Ph: Claire Richardson.
Page 39 The home of Jette Riis and Lars Hansen on Romo Island, Denmark.
Ph: Sus Rosenquist.
Page 40a/b Stola Herrgård, Sweden www.stola.se.
Page 41al The home of Ingegerd Raman and Claes Söderquist's home in
Sweden. Ph: Paul Ryan.
Page 42–44 (except 42b) Stola Herrgård, Sweden www.stola.se.
Page 45 Ph: Mark Scott.
Pages 46–59 Stola Herrgård, Sweden www.stola.se.
Page 60 Aki Wahlman's summer home in Finland. Ph: Paul Ryan.
Page 61 An apartment in The San Remo on the Upper West Side of
Manhattan, designed by John L. Stewart and Michael D'Arcy of SIT.
Ph: Andrew Wood.
Page 62 Mark and Sally of Baileys Home and Garden's house in Herefordshire.
Ph: Debi Treloar.
Page 63a The home of the designer Virginia Armstrong of
www.roddyandginger.co.uk.
Page 63bl Ph: Tham Nhu-Tran.
Page 63br Target Gallery, London. Ph: Thomas Stewart.
Page 64a The home of Tim Rundle and Glynn Jones. Ph: Debi Treloar.
Page 64b The home of the designer Virginia Armstrong of
www.roddyandginger.co.uk.
Page 65al The home of Tim Rundle and Glynn Jones. Ph: Debi Treloar.
Page 65ac An apartment in The San Remo on the Upper West Side of
Manhattan, designed by John L. Stewart and Michael D'Arcy of SIT.
Ph: Andrew Wood.

Page 65ar Ian Chee's apartment in London, chair courtesy of Vitra. Ph: Andrew Wood.

Page 65b The Home of Andy Marcus and Ron Diliberto in Palm Springs, CA. Ph: Andrew Wood.

Page 66 Jo Shane, John Cooper and family, apartment in New York. Ph: Andrew Wood.

Page 67l Ph: Martin Norris.

Page 67r The Finn Juhl house in Charlottenlund, Denmark. Ph: Andrew Wood. Finn Juhl's house is today a museum and part of Ordrupgaard. It is open to the public on weekends from 11.00 a.m.–4:45 p.m.; in June, July, and August it is also open Tuesday 1.00 p.m.–4:45 p.m., Wednesday 1.00 p.m.–6:45 p.m., and Friday 1.00 p.m.–4:45 p.m. http://ordrupgaard.dk/topics/collection-and-architecture/finn-juhl's-house.aspx

Pages 68–79 The home of the designer Virginia Armstrong of www.roddyandginger.co.uk.

Page 80 The home of James Russell & Hannah Plumb, the artists behind JAMESPLUMB www.jamesplumb.co.uk. Ph: Debi Treloar.

Page 81 The home of photographer and interior decorator Janice Issitt.

Page 82 and 83b The home of designer Niki Jones in Glasgow's West End. Ph: Debi Treloar.

Page 84 Ph: Andrew Wood.

Page 85al The cabin of Hanne Borge and her family in Norway. Ph: Catherine Gratwicke.

Page 85bl The family home of the stylist Anja Koops and chef Alain Parry in Amsterdam. Ph: Polly Wreford.

Page 86l The family home of Lea Bawnager, Vayu Robins & Elliot Bawnager-Robins, owner of affär. Ph: Debi Treloar.

Page 86r The London home of Sam Robinson, co-owner of "The Cross" and "Cross the Road." Ph: Debi Treloar.

Pages 88–101 The home of photographer and interior decorator Janice Issitt.

Page 102 Ph: Mark Lohman.

Page 103 The home of Madeline Tomlinson of Weathered and Worn.

Page 104 The home of Jeanette Lunde. Frydogdesign.blogspot.com. Ph: Debi Treloar.

Page 105a/b Ph: Mark Lohman.

Page 106 Ph: Mark Lohman.

Page 107b The home of photographer and interior decorator Janice Issitt.

Page 109l/r The home of photographer and interior decorator Janice Issitt.

Page 109c Ph. Simon Brown.

Pages 110–125 The home of Madeline Tomlinson of Weathered and Worn.

Pages 126–127 The French home of artist Alex Russell Flint.

Page 128 The home in Provence of Carolyn Oswald. Ph: Polly Wreford.

Page 129b Chateau de Christin, Chambres d'Hotes de Luxe, Reception—Seminaires. Ph: Claire Richardson.

Page 130a The London home of Shane Meredith and Victoria Davar of Maison Artefact. Ph: Claire Richardson.

Page 130b Amanda Pratt, Creative Director, Avoca Ph: James Fennell.

Page 131 Ph: Mark Lohman.

Page 132a Paul & Claire's beach house, East Sussex. Design www.davecoote.com; Location to hire through www.beachstudios.co.uk. Ph: Polly Wreford.

Page 132b Ph: Martin Norris.

Page 133r The French home of artist Alex Russell Flint.

Pages 134–149 The French home of artist Alex Russell Flint.

Page 152 Designer Barbara Davis' own house in upstate New York.

Page 154 Designer Barbara Davis' own house in upstate New York.

Page 155 The Jacomini Family Farm, designed by Jacomini Interior Design. Ph: Simon Upton.

Page 156 Compound by a lakeside in the mountains of western Maine designed by Stephen Blatt Architects. Ph: Jan Baldwin.

Page 157 Ph: Mark Lohman.

Pages 158–171 The family home of Rob and Jane Slater, Derbyshire.

Pages 172–173 Ph: Mark Scott.

Page 174a Ph: Mark Scott.

Page 174b The family home of Rob and Jane Slater, Derbyshire.

Page 175al/ac Ph: Simon Brown.

Page 175bl/bc Ph: Mark Scott.

Page 175ar/br The family home of Rob and Jane Slater, Derbyshire.

Page 177b Ph: Martin Norris.

Page 178 The family home of Rob and Jane Slater, Derbyshire.

Page 179l Ph: Mark Scott.

Pages 180–195 The home of the photographer Paul Massey in Cornwall.

Page 196 The cabin of Hanne Borge and her family in Norway. Ph: Catherine Gratwicke.

Page 198a Mark & Sally Baileys home in Herefordshire. Ph: Debi Treloar.

Page 198b The family home of the designer Emily Gray of www.gray-label.com.

Page 200 The home of James Russell & Hannah Plumb, the artists behind JAMESPLUMB www.jamesplumb.co.uk. Ph: Debi Treloar.

Page 202 The family home of the interior designer Larissa van Seumeren in the Netherlands. Ph: Catherine Gratwicke.

Page 203 Mathilde Labrouche of Cote Pierre's home in Saintonge. Styled by Mark & Sally Bailey. Ph: Debi Treloar.

Pages 204–215 The family home of the designer Emily Gray of www.gray-label.com.

INDEX

acknowledgments

As usual, a book is not done without a lot of help from many people. We would like to give a big shout-out to all the stockists of Annie Sloan paint and products all over the world for their ideas and thoughts about style. The idea for this book came through thinking about them and asking them to describe their own businesses.

Special thanks go to those who helped on individual projects: to Nick and Jenny Carr, from Vintage & Paint (www.vintageandpaint.com) for their help with the warehouse section, particularly their vintage lighting; to Claire and Spike Chalkley for their help with painting in France, and for being there when we needed you, and to Les Couronnes Sauvages (www.lescouronnessauvages.com) for their help with pulling together the idea of a flower choice and arrangement for each of the styles.

Thank you to the Annie Sloan team in the UK for all the magnificent help given to us and for rallying when we were frantic—especially Tanya Evans, who organized us all with such calmness.

A huge thanks to James Harrison for outstanding contributions throughout! And to Christopher Drake, for all the care and thought over our photography, and for the long days, too.

Finally to our families, especially Lizzy, Willow, and David, a big huge THANKS!

Neoclassical

Traditional Swedish

Modern Retro

Bohemian

Vintage Floral

French Elegance

Rustic Country

Coastal

Warehouse